# How to Get Invited
## to the
# WHITE HOUSE...

# How to Get Invited to the WHITE HOUSE

and Over One Hundred
Impressive Gambits, Foxy Face-Savers
and Clever Maneuvers

★ ★ ★

## JAMES C. HUMES

THOMAS Y. CROWELL COMPANY
*Established 1834 / New York*

*Designed by Eve Kirch Callahan*

Manufactured in the United States of America

Library of Congress Cataloging in Publication Data

Humes, James C
   How to get invited to the White House ... and over
   one hundred impressive gambits, foxy face-savers, and
   clever maneuvers.

   1.   Success.   I.   Title: How to get invited to the
White House ...
BJ1611.2.H85    131'.32    77-7640
ISBN 0-690-01658-1

77 78 79 80 81 10 9 8 7 6 5 4 3 2

*To my late cousin*
*Bill Graham*
*and my older brother*
*Graham Humes*
*who both inherited the*
*Graham love of fun and*
*adventure*

# Acknowledgments

First, I would like to thank for the arduous task of reading my handwriting Nadja Gill as well as my long-time assistant Stephanie Laszlo.

Then, there are numerous other people who have been helpful in various ways: Lord Crathorne, Carpenter Dewey, Barbara Gillam, Jane Krumrine, Victor Lang, John LeBoutillier, Charles Manatt, Ken Talmage, Ann Reilly, Sir John Wedgwood, Robin West, and Morris Wolff.

Finally, I am grateful to Faith Brunson, whose advice triggered the idea of the book as well as to the thousand book buyers and sellers who manifested their faith in my book by signing my petition for best seller.

# Contents

# Introduction: "Go Soak Your Head"

In the early years of the Kennedy Administration a girl who had just transferred from a job in the Pentagon to one in the White House confided in me that she was disappointed. Having forsaken the dull but regular employment of military administration for the long, hectic hours of work under the spotlights of Camelot, she had at least expected to be caught up in the edges of Washington's social whirl(pool?).

But alas and alack, the lass's social blue chips remained uncashed. She hadn't been whirled in a month of Sundays. She said, "Jamie, I might as well be working in an insurance office."

I stroked my chin, recalling the many times I'd been in and out of the White House during the Eisenhower years, and mulling over what I had heard about the new President's habits. "Okay," I said. "You know the women's powder room on the ground floor?"

"The one right near the swimming pool?"

"That's right." (Nixon had the pool converted to a bowling alley; psychology buffs may have a neat time wondering what that means.) "Every morning on your coffee break, say around 10:30, go down to that powder room, fill a basin with water, and soak your head. Not for too long. Half a minute will do fine. Then shake your hair out, dry it a little—but not completely—and put a scarf or something over it. When you go back to your office, don't answer any questions, and don't tell anybody where you've been."

"What's the idea?"

I smiled and shrugged. "Magic. Try it."

So she did. Two weeks later we had lunch together. She almost inhaled her martini, she was so breathless. "Jamie, I don't know what you're trying to do to my hair, but I've got the biggest case of the

xiii

frizzies and the most crowded social calendar of my life. A Colonel from the Joint Chiefs of Staff called me, and a Congressman. I've seen a really charming military attaché from the French Embassy a couple of times. The thing I can't understand is, people keep asking me about the President. 'Is the strain of office telling on him? How's his back?' And last night the military attaché asked me, 'What does he think of NATO?' " I said, 'He's for it.' What do I know? I just tell them what I read in the papers. But they're still fascinated. What's going on? Most of those people see the President more often than I do."

I smiled and shrugged. "You do work in his house, you know."

"I suppose."

I don't know whether she ever heard that the President frequently swam nude in that pool. Jackie never went near it. Only a few of his closest companions ever joined him, and rumor had it that not all were male.

The moral of this little story is simple. You may not have a job in the White House; only about five hundred people do. But wherever you are, if you just play your cards right, you can do a whole lot of things that not only will be a lot of fun, but will also impress your friends, get you out of personal dilemmas with style, or display your ingenuity and imagination. Most often it's not a huge change in your personality, your life-style, or whatever, that will make the difference between fantasizing and doing what strikes your fancy, but simply knowing the "how it's done"—little tricks of the trade that may or may not be common knowledge among "the initiated," but which, when added to your personal arsenal of experience and common sense and resources, will make things that once looked not-worth-the-trouble, or even impossible, seem easy.

The examples given in this book are just that—examples. They've been picked out of a list of more than three hundred candidates for inclusion because each one contains a little mini-moral you can extend to all kinds of other situations. For instance, if you want to get invited to a dinner at the Governor's mansion instead of at the White House, it should be easier, but the same basic strategies will apply.

I've used a lot of Washington examples in this book, not only because that's the scene I know best, but because Washington is a typical "seat of power" and a port-of-entry to the society of the world. Now, personally, I can't stand Washington, because it's full of people with no sense of humor; people who can't laugh at themselves. Washington is Hollywood East—all façade. Except that in Hollywood the name of the game is glamour, and in Washington it's power. The nation's capital is full of actors pretending to be serious about "the issues" who really couldn't care less about anything but their own status and egos. I frankly would rather have told a lot of *them* to go soak their heads.

But still, the really stylish power-play has its inescapable charm, and if you don't let style go to your head, you may as well take advantage of knowing "how it's done." After all, everyone else who knows does. And even if you don't find a single thing you'd want to do in these pages (in which case experience tells me you're a Martian), I trust you'll get a few hours of amusement out of knowing how numerous bigwigs undoubtedly "got theirs."

# How to Get Invited
## to the
# WHITE HOUSE...

# Get Invited to the White House

If you thought you could get invited to the White House, say for a state dinner, would you give it a try? After all, you're paying your share for the spreads they put on there, so you've got a right to be halfway curious about what they're like. And in case you've got a friend who keeps lording it over you that the Mayor shook his hand at the last Lion's Club picnic, a White House invitation might prove a handy equalizer.

The fact is that White House invitations, as impressive as they may be to most people, are not all that impossible to come by. Every year the White House hosts scores of dinners honoring foreign dignitaries on state visits, as well as special fetes like those President Nixon threw for Andrew Wyeth, Duke Ellington, and others. For most of these occasions, the White House social secretary must fill close to a hundred seats. And although a fair number will be taken up by the guest of honor's entourage and various government officials, a healthy percentage may still go to citizens from around the country who have presented themselves as the right Americans to throw into the mix.

Just as publishers are always looking for new material to fill out their seasonal lists, so the White House social secretary is always looking for likely guests for White House functions. So if a letter offering your services happens to be on the desk of Gretchen Poston, currently President Carter's social secretary, at the right time, you just might be on your way to an engagement at 1600 Pennsylvania Avenue, Washington, D.C.

Now of course you don't just write to the social secretary and ask to be invited to *a dinner,* as though you planned to be hungry some evening and wanted to stop by the restaurant. You have to plan your strategy a few months in advance. Your first step is to find out the White House social schedule for the time period you're interested in.

One way you can spot upcoming events for which you might be a

1

likely candidate is to follow the newspapers, where visits of foreign dignitaries and other major White House functions are announced months in advance. Another way is to call the White House, (202) 456-1414, ask for the social secretary's office, and inquire what state dinners are scheduled, say, from January to June. Either way, you will learn who is to be honored at each occasion.

Now—what possible connection do you have with the guests of honor, their countries, organizations, personal lives, etc.?

If you once met Canadian Prime Minister Eliot Trudeau at a ski resort, if you went to school with Prince Olaf's sister, if your husband does a lot of business in Spain, or if you are the head of your city's Alliance Française, you may already have what the social secretary is looking for. This kind of built-in pipeline to the guest of honor is a natural ticket to an invitation, especially when the guest of honor is not a leading international figure, but (like the heads of state of the newer and smaller countries) is himself invited to the White House primarily as a matter of protocol. If you don't yet have such pipelines and would like to get them, almost every other entry in this book will help you do that, but the ones immediately following will be the most helpful. Not that all pipelines lead to the White House dinner table, but many can be diverted in that direction.

At any rate, if you write to the social secretary and mention that you've learned there's to be a state dinner for Mr. X on Y date, that you were planning a trip to Washington around that time, that you have a special interest in X (or his country, cause, etc.) because ————, and that you'd be more than happy to help entertain him, you will be high in the running for a seat at the table (as long as you allow a few weeks at least to make a security check). And if you don't make it to the table, you stand an even better chance of being invited to the entertainment afterward, since there's room for at least two hundred more bodies in the East Ballroom . . . which means two hundred more job-slots for the social secretary to fill.

If you once had your picture taken with the guest of honor, had your name printed in connection with his, or whatever, your application will be greatly strengthened if you send a copy along as a "reminder." Also include a few basic facts about yourself, such as that you're forty-three years old, vice-president of Whiplash National Insurance Company, an active member of your local Chamber of Commerce, etc., just so they'll know you're for real. Such personal information often goes nicely in a

PS—as though you were about to seal your letter when you realized that although the guest of honor might be terribly interested in you, and may even know you personally, of course the White House social secretary can't be expected to know you and should be provided with a few basic facts about you for her files.

The key variable in getting invited to the White House is the special interest you have in the guest of honor (his country, his cause, etc.). You may have a special interest in Queen Elizabeth's country because you worked closely with the Royal Air Force high command during the war. You may have a special interest in Dahomey because you've learned that your ancestors were slaves imported from there, or because you just read about it someplace. But the reverse isn't true. Your special interest in a large and historically influential country like England can't be simply that you've learned that your ancestors came from there, or that you just read about it someplace. The moral is that the more momentous the state visit or occasion, the more "special" your interest must be. So if your hooks into the guest of honor or his affiliations aren't too strong, the guest had better not be too big a fish either.

But whether you were in one of Golda Meir's grade-school classes in Milwaukee or you once wrote a seminar report on Sri Lanka, you have to remember that you're making a competitive bid to fill a vacancy you think it would be worth your time to fill, and you should use a little imagination in realizing what your qualifications to fill that seat actually are. If you waited on tables at the first nightspot Ellington ever played, or if you bought Andrew Wyeth's first paintings, you were virtually passing up White House invitations when you didn't offer your presence at White House events honoring these people. The point is that a lot of seats at White House dinners go to the highest bidders, and what does it cost you to make a bid?

Sometimes not getting a White House invitation is more valuable than getting one. Not too many people know it, but the infamous Nixon "enemies list" started out as a list of "Guess Who's Not Coming to Dinner." Back in the days of spirited attacks on Presidents, unsophisticated White House staffers managed to let a few prime personæ non gratæ slip onto invitation lists. After the hues and cries of "Who the hell invited *him?*" died down in the White House halls, someone thought it would be a good idea to *write down* who ought to be scratched off automatically. In this case the executive's wish to Make Things Perfectly Clear and the subordinates' desire not to do anything Unautho-

3

rized proved a disaster, because it violated the cardinal rule of politics, which is Never Write Your Blacklist Down.

But, as history proved, a line on the blacklist was worth two seats at a dinner (at least). By the time Watergate was overflowing, people were getting themselves on the "Guess Who's Not Coming to Dinner" list as favors. One reporter I helped gain a line for (and who would never have been considered for a White House invitation anyway) rests most of his reputation on it to this day.

All Presidents have their blacklists, and if you happen to be on President Carter's current list, you've wasted your time reading so far. For instance, if you're Jerry Brown, you know damned well why you weren't invited to the state dinner honoring the first visit of the new President of Mexico . . . and any halfway conscious American who followed the presidential elections knows too. It doesn't matter that you're the Governor of the nation's most populous state, which just happens to border on Mexico. The Governors of New Mexico, Arizona, and Texas got invited, but you didn't—just because the President didn't wish the pleasure of your company. The average reader, however, stood a better chance of getting invited to the White House than the Governor of California. That's politics.

Although dinners are the most prestigious events to which you might be invited, there are also numerous receptions, afternoon teas, and other functions given by the First Lady to honor people or organizations as she chooses and to repay social and political debts. If the President stayed in your home somewhere along his campaign trail, he has probably already repaid you with an invitation. If you are in a position to do the First Family a favor now—if you live in or near Washington or can go there regularly, and can offer to help with such things as addressing thank-you notes or Christmas cards—get in touch with your Congressman and have him convey your offer to volunteer to the social secretary. If your offer is accepted, the Carters will undoubtedly convey their thanks through a White House invitation.

What happens if you feel you simply *have* to be invited to a certain White House dinner? Not many people feel that strongly about it, but during the Ford administration I got a frantic call from a lawyer friend who'd been put on the spot to come up with an invitation to a dinner honoring the Queen of England for the head of a large corporation. The corporation was the law firm's biggest client, so my friend couldn't tell its president to go float his own barge. Instead he called me. "This isn't a question of doing my best," he told me. "I've got to come up with that engraved square of cardboard."

The White House social secretary was an old colleague of mine (yet another way to get White House invitations is to know somebody who knows the social secretary), so I gave her a call.

"Impossible," she said. "Unless somebody dies." The invitations to the dinner honoring Queen Elizabeth had already been sent out. There wasn't a free seat in the dining room. Things had plainly gone beyond the mortal power of mere personal favors.

When I reported back to my lawyer friend he asked about the price of a murder contract on one of the lesser guests, but fortunately we were saved the indignity of assassination by my Columbus-like recollection that there might well be a backward route to this particular India. My friend was actively contemplating the comparative merits of suicide and murder when I interrupted him: "Wait a minute. The Queen will be giving her own banquet at the Embassy a night or two before the White House dinner."

"So what?"

"So she's also visiting Williamsburg before that."

"*So what!*"

"So your client has a lot of money, right? And he's willing to put out a hunk to get invited to the White House?"

"Right. But I don't get it."

"So what? Have your client offer Williamsburg some rare antique to commemorate the Queen's visit there. Make it the finest Georgian silver service he can lay his hands on."

Williamsburg always likes Georgian silver, and royalty always likes to be commemorated. So the businessman made his presentation, and the Queen naturally had him included on the guest list for her Embassy's banquet. When a comparison of her list with the White House's showed he had somehow been omitted from the latter, a White House invitation was hastily issued.

Now this particular businessman paid a lot for his invitation, and you might well wonder whether a White House dinner—hardly the most rollicking bash of all time—was really worth it, even for him. That's a question I leave to you, with the PS that just being able to tell people firsthand how bloody dull a White House dinner is might well be worth the price of your ticket.

# Get Your Name on Embassy Invitation Lists

You already know one way to get invited to an Embassy from the preceding pages, which is to offer something expensive to commemorate something important that someone important in that country does (such as the Queen's going out to have a look at the way part of her erstwhile colony used to be). But of course there are a lot more methods, and they come a lot easier and cheaper.

Some years ago a friend of the family asked if I would help out a young lady who had recently moved to Washington. She liked her government job, but unfortunately she was stricken with an all-too-familiar lament: the city she had expected to be glamorous, to dazzle her with splendid Embassy dinners and fascinating diplomatic receptions, had so far disincluded her in its social life.

I gave the young lady a call and, after passing the usual amenities about families and so on, broached the subject of her social predicament. She assured me it was as dire as I'd heard, so I prescribed some engraved calling cards and a phone call to me when she got them. When next I heard from her I invited her to deck herself out in a suit, hat, and gloves the following Saturday and meet me at noon in front of the Mayflower Hotel. And when the appointed day dawned bright and sunny, I hired a chauffeured limousine and swooped her up.

Up and down Sixteenth Street and Massachusetts Avenue we drove, stopping at each Embassy. The chauffeur would open the door for my young friend with much ceremony, and she would demurely mount the steps and ring the bell of the Ambassador's residence. When the doorman answered, she would recite, "I would like to pay my respects to His Excellency, the Ambassador of ———, and to the people of ———," meanwhile dropping her card onto the silver tray kept in the foyer for just such purposes.

We did this seventy times that afternoon at seventy Embassies. By the time we were through she was mumbling under her breath, "I would like to pay the Ambassador to respect my excellency . . . I would like to suspect the excellency of paying the Ambassador. . . ." But in the next few months she received about twenty Embassy invitations. As I had expected, there were no invitations to dinners at the British or French Embassies in that first batch, but she did get invited to a lot of cocktail parties at the Embassies of the newer African and Asian nations, where she met a number of diplomats from other countries and gained new footholds in the social circles she'd been so curious about.

Now if you happen to live in Washington State instead of Washington, D.C., but would like to make contact with foreign Ambassadors and get invited to Embassy functions when or if you do happen to go to the nation's capital, there is of course a way. Take out your handy-dandy, up-to-the-minute map of the world and plunk your finger down on some small country you have visited, studied about, or whatever. Then ask yourself what local group might invite the Ambassador, Counselor of the Embassy, or even Cultural Attaché of that country to come and speak.

Whether you belong to the group or not, you make the initial contact and handle all the arrangements with the Embassy. If you give plenty of time for scheduling, invite your diplomat to speak on some topic general enough to allow him to say what he wants—and don't invite the Turkish Ambassador to speak to the Greek-American Club, etc.—your invitation will in all probability be accepted.

Now the real fun begins. You provide the speaker with a little background—a page or so—on the group he'll be speaking to. You send him clippings about his country that have appeared in local publications. (This is a service Embassies especially appreciate.) You offer to arrange a comfortable place for him to stay if he'd rather not bed down in a hotel. You pick him up at the airport, perhaps show him a few sights, brief him a little more, and see that his visit goes smoothly and pleasantly. After he leaves, you write and thank him for his speech, enclose newspaper clippings about it (of course you alerted the newspapers beforehand), and continue to send him clippings. When appropriate, ask if you could be of assistance in writing a letter to the editor on some subject related to his country.

By this time you will already be on the Embassy invitation list, and

your next trip to Washington, D.C., will definitely include being enter-
tained at the Embassy, whether you've made the trip especially for that
purpose or have just mentioned that you'll be in D.C. at such-and-such a
time. And if you're planning a vacation or other trip to his country,
don't hesitate to let him know. You should be in for a little stately
treatment there, too.

By the way, the Embassies of Communist countries are as happy as
any, and perhaps happier, to issue invitations or send representatives to
speak to local groups; but you should remember that a place on their
invitation list might also get you a place on an FBI list. That doesn't
bother me, but it may bother you.

# Become a Diplomat Without Leaving Home

You don't have to apply for the foreign service or give millions to the
campaign fund of a winning presidential candidate to become a diplomat. (New election finance laws have made the campaign-contribution
route all but impossible anyway.) If you live in a major city (preferably
one with an important harbor), if you have some time to give to things
diplomatic, and especially if you have your own office to work out
of—a law office, a real estate brokerage, etc.—you have the material
for a consulate.

Since a Consul (nowadays, anyway) is an official appointed by a
government to represent a country's commercial or other interests in a
foreign land, it stands to reason that you are not going to be a U.S.
Consul in New Orleans. So whose Consul are you going to be? Well,
you are going to be some other country's *honorary Consul*—
representing that country with a local office as a convenience for those
in your community.

The work which is strictly volunteer, largely involves helping people
with papers (American businessmen who want to trade with the country

you represent, people with visa or other problems, etc.) and contacting the Embassy for instructions when you need to. It helps if you know the language of the country you represent, but even that is not necessary. Small countries especially appreciate having honorary Consuls in cities like Philadelphia, Denver, Chicago, or Milwaukee.

So if you think you might be interested in becoming a diplomat, an inquiry sent to your favorite country's Embassy in Washington will tell you what you need to know. If your father was born in Sweden or if you've done a lot of business in Uruguay, those countries will be "naturals" for you. If you've already got ties with some Embassy, so much the better; honorary Consul status certainly won't hurt them. Along the way you should meet a lot of interesting people, get invited to a lot of good parties, and learn a lot about the country you've "adopted." Often an honorary Consul receives a sash to wear at white-tie functions or a rosette or other badge of office—which will mean you won't have to shudder if you receive formal invitations which read "decorations and insignias will be worn." And perhaps after some years of service the Order of Bolivar or some similar medal will be bestowed upon you. It will really dress up your dinner jacket. A friend of mine who became an honorary Consul got himself DPL (diplomatic) license plates for ten dollars and a request to the Motor Vehicles Department. As residents of such cities as New York and Washington know, DPL plates are magic charms against parking tickets.

# Become a Famous Washington Hostess

In Washington, D.C., where one might expect society to be extremely exclusive and "tight," it is surprisingly easy to become a famous hostess—if you have the first prerequisite, which is money in large amounts. If you have money, you don't need to have a famous name, be married to a Senator or an Ambassador, look beautiful, be witty, or have any grandiose political, diplomatic, or social connections. Money is all Perle Mesta and Gwen Cafritz started with, and they ended up as the most renowned hostesses of the Truman and Eisenhower eras. Perle was just the widow of a wealthy oil man, and Gwen the wife of a wealthy Washington realtor. Yet virtually every important U.S. Senator, key Cabinet official, influential Ambassador, and Supreme Court Justice in Washington ended up at their homes as dinner guests, along with Presidents of the United States.

Now, naturally anyone with a lot of money and the sense to pick up a telephone can get a dinner catered and served, a door answered by a butler, and drinks mixed by a bartender. But in most cities this is not going to land at your door the Rockefellers, Vanderbilts, their more modern counterparts, or whomever you please. In general, private citizens go only where their whims or their businesses take them, which is usually in pretty exclusive circles. In all cities the rule holds that if you can throw a party for a famous enough person, the local lights will turn out in droves. But only in Washington (and to a lesser extent in New York, using UN diplomatic circles) can you count on "snowballing"—starting with a "minor" guest and working up to the bigger ones. It works through protocol, which dictates most of what diplomats do.

As a budding Washington hostess your first guest of honor might be a newspaper columnist (only in D.C. does a columnist rank somewhere between a U.S. Congressman and a U.S. Senator) or politician or labor leader or movie star—if you can land one of these. But if you can't, never forget the Ambassadors from the smaller countries. If you go over to the Kennedy Center for the Performing Arts on any Sunday afternoon when the Washington Redskins are playing in town, you will find a high concentration of diplomats oblivious to the difference between a screen pass and a trapblock but listening with rapt attention to a string quartet. Half the audience may well be diplomats. So, during intermission or after the concert is over, you start a conversation about the music, the weather, or whatever, and turn the talk to the Ambassador's country. Perhaps you inquire about its national holidays; or if you've done a little homework, you may know the major ones already. At any rate, you are trying to find the right occasion to honor his country with a dinner, a reception, or whatever, at which he can be the guest of honor.

Once you have hit on the occasion, the idea occurs to you that since you often give large parties and receptions, you might want to make the next one extra-special, and would he like to be the guest of honor? If he says no at this point, he's either too big a fish for the moment or a very eccentric Ambassador, and you try someone else. But sooner or later, you'll get your guest of honor.

Now comes the snowballing. Who would the Ambassador like invited? Does he know Sir Peter Ramsbotham, the British Ambassador? Would he like him on the list? Are the French or Iranian Ambassadors (the Iranian Embassy is the hottest thing on the 1977 Embassy Circuit) friends of his?

You take the names he suggests, call the most impressive one first, and say you are having a party for Ambassador Upstart on the occasion of Upstartia's Independence Day, and would he like to come? If he can't make the date you've suggested, change it. Your party probably won't fall exactly on Upstartia's Independence Day anyhow, because the Embassy will probably host its own informal reception then.

Once you have a commitment from your most influential prospect, the party should start to take shape. If it was the Italian Ambassador you landed, you can call the French Ambassador, and with his acceptance you may get the British. Now, on the basis of Ambassadors who may be coming out of diplomatic respect and courtesy (protocol), Senators will start accepting your invitations because their wives want to meet the Ambassadors, and Cabinet Secretaries will come because they have things to talk over with Senators.

The Washington hostess doesn't provide entertainment for her guests; she simply provides an elegant informal setting for discussions. A Senator once told me that more phone calls are generated by an evening at a party than by a whole day's contacts with constituents. What sets Washington parties apart from most others is that Ambassadors, Senators, Cabinet Secretaries, etc., will come to the homes of people they have never met or even heard of, simply as a matter of protocol, or because of who else will be there. Only in Washington could someone like Carl Albert come to a buffet dinner I once gave for young Winston Churchill, grandson of the late Prime Minister, and, midway through the proceedings, lean over and whisper into my ear, "Who's this guy Humes that's giving the party?"

One final tip on greeting guests as a superhostess, which Perle Mesta confided to me in 1969. President Truman had rewarded her loyalty to the Democratic Party by making her Ambassador to Luxembourg, and

11

after a party at the Embassy there, I asked her to divulge her wisdom on this matter. "Honey," she boomed, "when each guest arrives, I give him a big hug and say, 'At last!' And when he leaves, I cry, 'Oh no, so soon?' "

# Contact Celebrities

If you have a legitimate reason to want to get in touch with a celebrity—any kind of celebrity at all, from a sports figure to a politician to an entertainer to a high-society type—you can usually do it on a few hours' notice. (Unless the celebrity happens to be in Afghanistan today, which you can also find out.)

Let's say you have something to offer a celebrity, especially in terms of money, publicity, etc., that's a legitimate reason to contact him. So before you decide he wouldn't be interested, go ahead and find out. One of the most common legitimate reasons to contact a celebrity is to ask whether he would be interested in doing a benefit for your favorite charity. If he likes the cause and is convinced the benefit is going to be well run, well attended, and get him a lot of good publicity, it's like money in the bank. If he's not booked up, why not do it?

Of course the best way to contact a celebrity is through some network of mutual acquaintances. But if you don't have those connections with celebrities, there are people who do, and make a business out of them. One is Earl Blackwell, whose Celebrity Service, in New York, publishes a Celebrity Guide listing the day-by-day itineraries of all famous actors, authors, musicians, statesmen, etc. Celebrity Guide costs about seven hundred dollars a year to subscribe to, but if you have a friend who works at a big public relations firm or advertising agency, or even better a theatrical or lecture agency, he may be able to give you the information you want.

If you want quick and personalized action, however, call Roz Starr, also in New York, at (212) 354-5050. She will make sure your purpose is legitimate and then, for five dollars a name, will either tell you immediately how to get in touch with the celebrity of your choice, or will track him down for you.

# Have Celebrities as Your House Guests

It is not as impossible as it might seem to invite famous people to stay in your home and have them accept. Williamsport, Pennsylvania, where I grew up, is a small upstate city that seems more midwestern than eastern, and its primary claim to fame is as the cradle of Little League baseball. Yet, when I was a boy, playwrights like Elmer Rice and pianists like Alec Templeton were overnight guests in our house. John Charles Thomas sang grace there, and Carl Sandburg read poetry.

I am not going to tell you that if you invite Elizabeth Taylor or Queen Elizabeth to spend the night some time, they'll come tooting out on the next train. People like that are constantly in the public eye and have no lack of hospitality or company; they are recognized wherever they go, and much of the time their problem is to get away. But people like authors and the more classical performing artists generally do not have those problems. They may be on the road performing, or lecturing, etc., a great deal of the time, without huge entourages—and when it comes to bedding down for the night, they're largely on their own.

When my mother learned that a celebrity she admired was coming to town, she got his address through the agency that had booked him and wrote him asking if he would like to stay in our home. I used to think the invitation was (often, anyhow) accepted just because the celebrity feared Williamsport's hotel accomodations wouldn't be adequate. But after a few years on the lecture circuit myself, I realized that hopping from hotel to hotel is incredibly boring. Staying in one indistinguishable Sheraton or Holiday Inn after another is like travelling and going no-place. It doesn't take long to wear out the "sights" of most towns, and the local people are what make the towns in the first place. It is depressing to go back to a lonely hotel room after pouring oneself out in some kind of performance, and authors, actors, and other celebrities generally agree that it is much nicer and more rewarding to stay in local people's homes.

This is not all there is to it, however. My mother was successful largely because her letters of invitation to celebrities showed three things. She was respectable (the wife of a Judge), she was bright (her letters were full of wit), and she would not exploit her guests. The last point is perhaps the most important. Mother's "celebrity guest" would not have the social obligations of the usual house guest. She offered him his own bedroom and bath and made it clear that he could come and go as he chose; she wouldn't spring twenty-five of her friends on him at a party planned around his presence.

By the same token, however, if you follow my mother's "formula" for celebrity house guests, you won't feel that you have to entertain them, fix them special dinners, or do the other things you might normally do—and on the whole, your celebrity guests would prefer that you didn't go to any special trouble. Perhaps that's because if you do, they start to wonder whether you're just doing it to get them to "repay" you in some way. That's an exploitive reason to *invite* anyone to anything, and they don't even know you yet.

My mother's understandings with her celebrity guests illustrate well what kinds of things they appreciate. She would let a guest know he could either eat breakfast with the family at 8:00 A.M., or she could bring coffee, orange juice, and toast up to him at whatever time he filled in on a note she left outside his door. He was on his own for lunch. If he got home by seven he was welcome to eat supper with us, but otherwise he was assumed to be dining out.

If a guest seemed especially congenial, as though he might enjoy meeting some more of the local folks informally, mother might invite a few friends over for supper. But she'd tell the guest: "A few people will be coming over tonight. I'm cooking up a big pot of spaghetti, and they're bringing Chianti. We're not expecting you, but of course you're invited. It's come-as-you-are, serve yourself." No hints of "These people are just dying to meet you," or "We *do* hope you'll come." But almost invariably they did come.

So if you see that a celebrity you admire is coming to town and you think he might appreciate staying in your home instead of a hotel, you have nothing to lose by tracking down an address where you can write to him offering your hospitality. Or if you want, you can stop by the local

TV studio when the guest of the day is on a talk show plugging his latest book and ask him. He may come—I know I have. Or you can offer to put up political candidates. In 1976 some people did just that with an unknown named Jimmy Carter, and they are now going to White House dinners.

My most vivid memory of our celebrity guests was of Carl Sandburg, who kept me awake singing along to his mandolin. I couldn't hear the words, but my mother told us later that most of the songs were bawdy.

# Get Your Name or Picture in the Paper

The only sure-fire way I know to get your name in the paper is to commit a criminal act so heinous that Vlad the Impaler would blanch at the details. Short of that, you might try running through the Boston Common naked or going over Niagara Falls in a barrel. All of these ruses, however, have been used before, and for those of you unwilling to imperil body and soul for the sake of publicity, it might be wise to investigate more mundane pathways to the front page.

First of all, look at your newspaper. What kind of things is it printing? Is there a column that your name might, without excessive manipulation, fit into? If you're a trout enthusiast with a new method for fly-tying, write the fishing editor. Or maybe the "Local News" spot would like to have a personal account of the big downtown fire you witnessed last week. If you've just given a reception for a girlhood chum who's published her first book of poetry, surely the society page should know.

If there's no slot you can easily fill, make one of your own. Create your own newsworthy event. This need not be as radical as streaking across the Boston Common. It can be as down-to-earth as your presentation to the local historical society of your Greataunt Minnie's crewel work, or your presentation to the Mayor of an early daguerreotype of the city.

Rummage through your attic and cellar. Those 1920s postcards that you always thought so crude might be just what your local library has been looking for. Surely a small ceremony can be arranged: just the librarian, the Mayor, and you. If you can't find anything more dramatic to present, write your Congressman and ask for a flag that's flown over the nation's Capitol. These are readily available. Great numbers of flags are hauled up and down every year for this very purpose—but the school, American Legion Post, or whatever other institution you present it to won't necessarily know or care about that.

Photographs are the newspapers' mainstay. Editors need them to break up the dreariness of solid newsprint, and there is a limit to the number of straight head shots they can use. So they are always on the hunt for action photos, for candids (or posed candids) with two or three people involved.

Dream up a situation that invites a photograph. The Aunt Minnie presentation would do fine. Or capitalize on one that already exists: that mailbox on your corner that the kids have painted flowers on, for instance. Invite a photographer to snap you at the appropriate moment (no one has to know you are paying her), and have her send the picture to the local gazette.

If you'd like to be quoted as well (and who doesn't?), you might invent an ad hoc committee focusing on some local issue and send the paper a press release: "Michael Spikehead, spokesman for the Committee to Abolish Everything Bad, today proclaimed that..." Suppose Hurricane Xena has just knocked down that stately old oak across the street. Announce yourself as the president of the Alliance Against Sloppy Summer Storms, and write the editor an irate denunciation of wandering low-pressure systems. Newspapers are always looking for fillers, and you never can tell what may come of it.

# Get on National Television

If you think it would be a kick to get on national television, but don't happen to have done anything lately to make the camera crews come running after you with maniacal greed in their lenses, you have several options.

One is to climb to the top of the nearest tall structure and threaten to throw yourself off if the major networks don't gather 'round immediately and start rolling up footage of your precious puss. This is not such a great idea, because if President Carter happens to announce on your chosen day that *he'll* throw *himself* off the top of the World Trade Center if the Russians don't start respecting human rights, the only coverage you'll get is a local newspaper photographer standing around on the street waiting to get a dynamite shot of you as you hit the pavement.

A better but more involved way to get on national TV is to get yourself a cause. During the eras of civil-rights and antiwar demonstrations, more "unknowns"—activists and organizers—got time on the tube than ever before or since. Especially if you can get yourself at the head of a lot of people who seem ready to tear something apart if something isn't done right away, whether it's getting someone famous out of jail or closing down the local porno shops (and if you alert the media beforehand, do your thing in some major city, and preferably schedule it at the TV crews' convenience, which usually means between 10:00 A.M. and 3:00 P.M. on a weekday), again, the lights of TV-land might just shine upon you.

But if all this seems like too much trouble for the reward of being able to say you were on national TV, all you really have to be willing to do is make a harmless idiot out of yourself on a game show. And who knows? Maybe you'll go back to Iowa with a thirty-seven-foot cabin cruiser in your back pocket.

17

One husband I know who wanted to get his wife an extra-special birthday gift hired a New York public relations firm for a few hundred dollars to get her on TV. The PR consultant had the husband write up a short biography of his wife, stressing such fun facts and humorous incidents as her birth on April Fool's Day, their first meeting on a blind date for a rodeo, her passion for ice cream with peanuts and marshmallow sauce, her pet racoon, and the time her wig fell off when she was doing the limbo with the featured performer in a Virgin Islands nightspot. That earthshaking material allowed the PR people to get her picked as a contestant in two Los Angeles game shows, with one talk show thrown in for good measure. In terms of fame in her own community, her husband's surprise gift was several million times better than a fur coat.

But of course you don't have to hire a PR firm to get yourself on game shows. All you have to do is contact the studio that produces the show (calling them up is best and fastest) and arrange to go in and take a test. If you don't think you'd be very good at naming all the uses of the peanut in twelve seconds, pick a show that only requires you to gush, exude, cry, gesticulate, screech, wail, fly into hysterics of joy, and collapse into the arms of the host—in between tremblingly pointing at some box, numbered square, or whatever, and saying that you picked the number nineteen because you have nineteen children.

If you think you can faint at the sight of a freezer or turn somersaults in front of a sable, you may well have a future in the national broadcasting of canned insanity. And of course if you keep your own sense of humor and perspective about it, you can tell your friends, "What a lark! It really was fascinating! The way they expect you to act! I should have got paid more than a lousy sable for my performance! I thought I was going too far when I tore the emcee's coat off his back, but afterward the producer said it was just perfect!"

If you would prefer to write the studios rather than call, pick your network and your show and fire off a letter. For NBC, write to NBC Tickets, 3000 West Alameda, Burbank, California 90515. For CBS it's 524 West Fifty-seventh Street, New York, N.Y. 10019. With ABC you have to write to the show itself; pick the producer's name off the list of credits at the show's end. Remember that for shows such as *Password* and *Concentration,* which involve some ad-libbing, your letter should show some wit and a sense of humor.

Keeping in mind the husband whose PR people also got his wife on a panel show—don't rule it out. It's true that you usually have to be famous or do something totally off the wall to get on a panel show, but a New York producer tells me that he, like most producers, keeps a file of "real people" to balance off his panels. Undoubtedly you have noticed, scattered in among movie stars, militants, Mafia hit-men in hoods, and the other colorful characters who regularly populate panel shows, the odd housewife from Keokuk with four children, who is manifestly there to lend a little common sense to the occasion. Naturally you can't just write a producer and say, "Hey, I'm Janet Average, so dub me a 'real person' and let me at those fruitcakes." But producers do tell me that if you write a balanced, well-reasoned letter taking issue with some unconventional position expressed in a recent program, it will end up in the "real people" file, and someday you just may get a call.

# Prepare for Talk Show Interviews

If you are appearing on a talk show for the first time, chances are it's on local TV or radio. The rules of preparation are much the same for regional or national shows, although if anything less preparation is generally needed there, because the host himself is probably better prepared, and because if you're picked for these shows you've probably already proven yourself to be an entertaining guest or dynamic speaker. But if you're in doubt as to how much preparation you need on any level—more is always better, so follow the game plan for local shows.

The first step is to forget any ideas you may have that the host will be so expert at his job, and so thoroughly briefed about your exhibit of watercolors at the Hoity-Toity Gallery or your new theory about why City Hall fell down, that all you have to do is take cues from him and you will come out looking or sounding good. Not so. The odds are great that the host has never read your book or heard your record and is not really dying to know all about it. He didn't pick you as a guest anyway

19

(the producer did) and now he's wondering how he can make a watercolor exhibit positively electrifying over the airwaves. Because if too many interviews are dull, then *he* is dull—and there goes his job.

Remember that you have been put on the talk show not because you or your subject is so absolutely fascinating, but because there are few well-known celebrities coming through town and the station cannot have the same local guests over and over; so the producer is ever-desperate for fresh material. It doesn't matter to him or the host whether you're a terrific biologist, football coach, or community organizer. It only matters whether you're a terrific talk show guest—because, with the possible exception of public television, TV and radio are still above all entertainment. If you are entertaining, provocative, etc., you'll soon move into the ranks of the people they think about often and ask, "Is it too soon to invite him back again?"

So your second step is to figure out what *you* want to say, which should almost always include something sensational or hilarious. Think of your most shocking disclosure on drug abuse, or remember the time you were painting that barnyard scene and the goat ate your tube of black paint (which explains why all the shadows in the picture are purple). If you have something to plug, figure out ways to work it in nicely but firmly. "If you'll go down to the Hoity-Toity Gallery on Main Street before next Friday and see my exhibit, you'll notice where the goat also bit a hunk out of the corner of my 'Study of a Silo and Manure Pile.' The farmer told me that for five dollars he could get the goat to eat the whole thing. I thought of taking him up on it and leaving a blank space in the exhibit over the caption, 'Painting Eaten by a Goat,' but the Hoity-Toity Gallery probably wouldn't have stood for it."

Once you know what you want to say, you can always work the conversation around to it, no matter what the interviewer's questions are. If your material is good, the host not only won't mind, he'll be grateful. You see, if he asks you a lame question like "Do you really think child abuse is on the rise?" he doesn't want you merely to say yes. That is his nightmare. Neither does he want you to reel off a whole set of boring or complicated statistics. He wants your most sensational disclosure. I gave this advice to a psychologist friend of mine who was later asked the above question on a show. She replied, "Well, your state reported seventeen cases of infant gonorrhea last year. What do *you* think?"

The ultimate in preparation, however, is to figure out what you want to say and then supply the host with a list of questions that will let you say it. Figure on two or three questions for each five minutes of a show, but don't expect them all to be asked; the list is for the host's convenience if he gets stuck and wants to make sure he asks you a question you have a good answer for. Preface your question list with a little introductory blurb which the host can, if he wants, read straight out onto the air:

"Dr. Smellington Smathers, our guest tonight, has cracked up the city with his prediction that if the city fathers and the inmates of the local insane asylum were to trade places for a month, the only noticeable differences would be a slight increase in governmental efficiency and a much more amusing political scene. I'm sure you've all read in the papers about Dr. Smathers' challenge to the Mayor that the experiment be given a try.

"Dr. Smathers—as an assistant professor of Governmental Pathology at Blathering University, and author of a highly acclaimed new book entitled *Why Blither?*—how serious are you about this idea?"

Of course, whether the host throws your prepared material into the garbage can or reads it off verbatim like a grocery list, you still have your answers, some of which you are going to use no matter what he asks.

If you are at all uncertain how you'll perform in answering your own questions, try a little "role-playing" beforehand. Get a friend to play the host, and maybe even a few others to listen. Your host-player should try you on your own questions and on throwing you off. Keep your eye on a clock so you get an idea of just how much can be done in a five- , a ten- , a fifteen- , a thirty-minute interview.

It will help a great deal if you have listened carefully to other of the host's shows and know whether he tends to be sympathetic to his guests or (as some are) hostile; whether he likes humor, scandal, practical advice to listeners, etc.; whether he tends to hold freewheeling discussions or seems to hold tightly to an agenda based on the guest's subject. If the latter is the case, he is very likely reading from a list of questions the guest has supplied.

And finally, when you go into the studio and the countdown to air time gets short—whether you've just spent half an hour with the host planning the interview or whether he's rushed in from East Noplace with a red face and lipstick on his collar—think of him not as some surreal character in a weird and foreign media-world, but as a new acquaintance you're going to talk with and entertain just as if he'd walked into your living room. You'll be a lot less nervous that way, and you'll be a lot better guest in the living rooms of the audience.

# Correspond with Famous Authors

Some years ago, while I was waiting for a young lady in her living room, I scanned the books on her coffee table and was fascinated to find a book of poetry by Robert Frost with a letter pasted inside the jacket. I must confess I read it. It was from the poet himself. Curious, I looked at the other books. James Michener, William Faulkner, John O'Hara, John Steinbeck—all contained personal letters from the authors.

I asked my friend how she had acquired her unique collection. Was she a lost daughter of Homer, with fabulous personal connections? No. It was simple. She had written to the authors, in care of their publishers, whose addresses were printed on the flyleaves of the books, and they had responded.

"You mean you just write to an author and ask him for a letter?" I was incredulous.

"No," she explained. "I usually ask some simple questions. For example, I asked John O'Hara where he got his perfect ear for conversation. Did he overhear things on the street and write them down for future use, or did he know instinctively how people talk in given situations?"

To a famous historical novelist, she had written: "Do you have a system for the historical research for your books? I know you often travel to location. Do you spend part of each day interviewing, part of it reading? I'm very interested in the patterns of your research."

"Don't any of them find this intrusive? Do most of them write back, or just a handful?"

"Oh," she assured me, "you'd be surprised how many authors are eager to correspond. They're not like movie stars, you know, continually badgered by autograph hounds. And anyway, all authors are egoists. They're flattered as hell to have somebody write them a letter and say, 'I really liked the book.' Yes, I'd say the great majority write back."

It helps, she explained, if you've actually read the author's book. It seems like the least you can do before starting up a correspondence with him, and it will enable you to phrase your questions with a little more precision than if you only read a review or a dustjacket blurb. If, for example, you should ask Isaac Asimov where he gets *his* ear for dialogue, or Betty Friedan how she plans her research, they will know you only want a letter to paste up on the coffee table, and they won't answer. Keep your letters brief, informal, and as personal as possible without becoming actually brazen. Keep in mind that you are addressing a Very Famous Person who seldom gets any attention. His contact with his audience is extremely limited. Often his publisher's sales figures are the only evidence he has that anybody outside of his neighborhood has ever heard of his books. He will expect to be treated with at least the modicum of dignity customarily accorded his profession, but beyond that he will be only too pleased to respond to a sincerely worded interest in his work.

One proviso is in order. Certain authors, such as John Updike, are extremely jealous of their privacy and are easily irked by importunities, however warmly intended, from the outside. It is best to stay away from such birds. This means that if no response to your initial query is forthcoming, you should probably forget it. There are, after all, plenty of authors around who will respond to a stranger's opening with gratitude and grace. It does not take long to say hello, and if you want to start your own collection of authors' letters, the opportunity is no further away than the nearest pen.

And who knows? One thing may lead to another. You may find yourself inundated by mail from lonely writers. You may not stop with one brief exchange. You may become pen pals forever, or even get to meet. Before long you might be tripping fabulously through the dazzling world of publishing lunches, movie contracts, and autograph parties. And all because of a simple note: "Hi. I liked your book."

# Become a Published Author

In the past year two acquaintances of mine had their first books published. One is a brilliant young woman whose fine academic record led her to a job on the White House staff; the other is a sixty-two-year-old grandmother who barely finished high school. Both books were on the same subject. Neither required much original or creative writing, or in fact much writing at all, because most of the material in both was plagiarized.

What was the subject?

Cooking.

Plagiarizing recipes for cookbooks is not only legal, it's necessary. There are very few recipes in the world that have never been published. So if you want the quickest and easiest way to get your name listed in the Library of Congress Index, be honored at an autographing party, get on radio or local TV talk shows, and so on, all you need is a catchy title and access to a lot of cookbooks. If you can work your own favorite recipes and techniques in, that's fine. Maybe your grandmother really did leave you that sheaf of priceless recipes. But the important thing is the title—the special theme of your book. So before you start collecting recipes in earnest, stop by a few bookstores and see what kinds of titles are around. You might even take down the names of some publishers while you're at it. Note what kinds of titles they're using, and start kicking similar kinds of titles around in your head and among your friends. Unless you're an expert, it's better to stay away from weight and nutrition subjects; instead, think of shortcuts (*The Three-Minute Gourmet*), regional or ethnic selections (*Cajun Cookery, Dinner for Danes*), special uses for foods (*The Versatile Turkey: 100 Recipes*), or books for people in special situations (a little humor always helps—how about *How to Cook What Your Husband Kills,* for the wives of hunters and fishermen?). Remember, writing cookbooks is not just a woman's occupation; most of the world's great chefs are men. Barbecue cookbooks are naturals for men, as are bartending guides and the like.

Although you may want your first book to be on something other than cooking, the fact that cookbooks are among the easiest to get published says something important about the whole book trade. A cookbook is a "how-to" book of a most ancient and universal kind, and "how-to" books (like this one!) are in many ways the bread and butter of the publishing business. Also called self-help books, they appeal to a wide range of readers who might or might not read other kinds of books, but who feel that being initiated into the secrets of doing things they've always wanted to do is well worth the price of a book. In practical terms, these books are meant to pay for themselves many times over, which is probably why many diversified publishing houses count on the "how-tos" for the basic profit margins that allow them to gamble on other, chancier titles—first novels, for instance. So if you have (or can put together) some special skill that a large or particularly avid segment of the book-buying population might want, think about a "how-to" book.

But suppose you *could* be the author of a book—*any* kind of book— only you just plain "can't write" for publication?

There is always the possibility of collaboration with someone who can: your research, information, reputation, or whatever, and his organization, style, and polish. You might collaborate with anyone from a local newspaper reporter to a highly professional "ghost writer," depending on the needs of your project. If your subject is strong enough and has enough commercial appeal, and if you are or can become the source of authoritative information about it, you should be able to get it published, whether it's by you alone or by you "with Joseph P. Ghost."

If you can convince a writer (or an agent, who can get you a writer) that your idea has potential, the writer will very likely make a tentative agreement with you that if your material gets published he will get some percentage of the proceeds (50 percent is "standard," but of course standards sometimes vary) and work with you to write up an outline and sample chapters. Many professional free-lance writers will do book outlines and twenty-five to fifty pages of text on speculation. It doesn't take very long and often is a good investment, because this material can be submitted to a prospective publisher, who may then agree to publish the book and put up some advance money for you both.

In some cases—if the writer is not sure the project is a good risk, for instance—you may, if you have the money, want to advance him a fee for working on the project with you. For $300–$1000 or so you can get an outline and sample chapters, and if the book sells you get your money back off the top of his cut. In still other cases you may want to pay a professional rewrite editor to rework a draft you've done, either of a partial or a complete book, for an hourly or a flat fee; then all the rights to it remain yours. Or you may want to pay him to write the whole book.

If you're in the market for ghost writers or rewrite editors, contact literary agents; many have young writers in their stables who are making their way up in the world through this kind of work, or others who make very good livings specializing in it. If that tack doesn't seem right, look around your neighborhood. Ask your bookseller whether any writers live in your community. If there is a college near you, ask the English professors. Maybe they even have aspiring-writer students who would fit your bill. Remember that if your submission is strong enough for a publisher to buy as you submit it, the publisher is prepared to have his own editors do the rest of the work needed to polish it up. It's the commercial potential of the idea, or your name and fame, or whatever, that ultimately will sell the book.

The moral of this story is that an author and a writer are often two very different beasts, and many authors are not writers. In fact, many books are written specifically to give "personalities" ways to capitalize on their public relations assets. If you are the world's greatest talk show guest—maybe you're a psychologist, maybe you're a famous hostess: who cares?—a publisher will probably do your book just because you've got a ready forum for advertising it. And your royalties on the book will make your appearances (in which you always plug the book) at least doubly worthwhile.

One more thing about submitting to commercial publishing houses: always get the name of a particular editor to which you can address your submission. Otherwise your manuscript will go onto the huge slush-pile of books that come in "over the transom" and end up on secretaries' or editorial assistants' desks, sometimes not to be sorted through for months. If you have any personal contacts with publishing houses or can get them, use them for all they're worth. If not, you can get names from *Writer's Market*, put out yearly by *Writer's Digest* magazine. This invaluable book will also tell you which publishing houses to submit to, how to go about it, and a whole raft of other vital information. Of course we are talking here about how to become an *author,* not a *writer*—but *Writer's Market* is actually an endless guide to how to get yourself published. And when you write to your chosen editor, try to use his first name somehow, even if it means mentioning that you met him at the last bookseller's convention (nobody can remember everyone he met at a bookseller's convention), or you once talked to him in a bar in New York, or whatever. At that time you mentioned something about this book, and he said he might be interested, so here it is. Once he has the manuscript he's going to judge it on its own merits anyway; all your white lie has done is to get someone with authority to accept or reject your book in under six months.

Now suppose you have a few thousand dollars to spend on becoming a published author, and you have a book idea or even a finished book which just won't sell to a commercial publisher. The book could be a novel that's been rejected a dozen times, or a book of poetry, or the history of your family—anything that only a very few people will be interested in. But you want to see the book in print, and even hope to be able to sell some copies.

This is the time to think about the "subsidy presses"—the ones you pay to produce your book. (Some are listed in *Writer's Market.*) This is *not* the way for an aspiring writer to go; subsidy presses are colloquially known as "vanity houses" in the book trade, where paying money to have one's work produced is evidence that a writer is not professional (salable) enough to get paid for what he writes. You will not actually be considered a "published author" by any accepted standards if you use a subsidy press. But you will legitimately be able to say that you've subsidized the publication of your book (if you have to mention it at all) because you thought it would be a worthwhile thing to have in print, or because you didn't agree with the standards of commercial publishing houses, and that anyone who might want to read what you have to say about ———— can order a copy from ————.

# Find a Title for Your Book

Somerset Maugham was as famous for the titles of his novels (*Cakes and Ale, Moon and Sixpence, Of Human Bondage*) as he was for the novels themselves. On that account, he was constantly being asked by aspiring writers to help them find the right titles for their creations.

On one occasion when an author was badgering him to read his book and suggest a title, Maugham came up with the perfect solution. "There's really no need for me to read the book," he assured his anxious persecutor. "Just tell me—does it have anything about drums in it?"

"No, no, nothing about drums."

"Well how about bugles?"

"No, not a single bugle."

"Fine, then. Call it *No Drums, No Bugles*."

The point of Maugham's advice is that the title need not have anything to do with the content of the book. One prolific author of my acquaintance runs through *Bartlett's* starting with the sections on the Bible and Shakespeare. That is probably how Maugham came up with *Cakes and Ale*.

# Become a Newspaper Columnist

Your own column! To those of us unfamiliar with newspaper publishing, this might seem an impossible dream. The weekly byline, the photo in the little box—it's inconceivable. You may be saying to yourself that the vast popularity of the Jack Andersons and Ann Landerses of the world is proof that Columnists Know Something We Don't.

Not so.

Your own newspaper column can be, in fact, no further away than your hometown editor's desk. Not every column in your local paper, after all, displays the verbal pyrotechnics of a Bill Buckley or a Joe Pyne. Few of them, indeed, give any indication that their authors even know where the Middle East is.

The secret here is simple: don't waste time trying to break down the walls of Gotham and become another Art Buchwald or Tom Wicker. Everybody inside there has been inside forever, and they intend to remain there. The New York *Times* is not hiring.

But a young woman I know recently landed a job writing a theater column for a small weekly in New Jersey. She submits a piece every two weeks or so on the latest Broadway musical, the road shows, and nearby student productions. The varied fare suits her intermittent theatergoing, and the job allows her to see plays free, since the paper, being poor, can only pay her in complimentary tickets.

How did my friend land this plum?

She looked through a few local papers, determined which one did not have a regular theater column, phoned to say that she'd been a drama major in college, and would they like to hire her?

And they said yes.

If you want your own column, stick with what you know and love. Don't try to sell any paper, no matter how small, a kettle of international fish—especially if the deepest water you've ever seen was in the

29

bathtub. Look to your own hobbies, interests, experiences. Maybe you've been collecting stamps since you were eight years old. Maybe you play the meanest rubber of bridge in three counties. Maybe neither. But everyone has something to sell. Your own genuine interest in your subject will make itself felt to your audience.

You don't have to be an expert to start with—certainly not an expert with words. If you communicate your own sense of the thing, your copy will be passed on to an editor who can polish it so the hidden shine comes out. That's what editors are for.

If you should object, "Every paper I know already has a theater column, and a gardening column, and a cooking column, and one for games," I would ask: "Certainly that does not exhaust the possibilities? What about your collection of 262 old 45 rpm records? There's no slot yet for rock 'n' roll. What about the three summers you spent at Cape Cod? Surely you can expand that, with a little thought, into a column called "New England Views" or a weekly squib on biology.

I'm not saying that all you have to do is pick up a phone and say, "Hi, I'm here." Perhaps there will be interviews. Perhaps you'll have to write a couple of sample columns before you're made editor in chief. But you have, in memory or fantasy, something you can share with others. Your only task is to find out what that is, and let fly.

Look in your own paper. You'll find a bewildering variety of personal columns, and the focus of not a few will be a trifle more eccentric than cooking, gardening, or trout fishing. Local views, for example, are very popular. One man I knew in a small Ohio town made a meager but comfortable living writing a weekly piece on local history. He was neither a professional historian nor a writer. All he had done was capitalize on a boyhood excitement for turning up Indian arrowheads, check a few books out of the public library, and start typing.

# Get Yourself on the Lecture Circuit

Perhaps you have been thinking for some time that your intimate knowledge of Chinese culture, criminal law, or how to get invited to the White House and over a hundred other things well qualifies you to run around the country like a lot of other people do, getting paid to speak on these topics. Your speaking style is scintillating, you are dynamic, positively fascinating—everybody says so. But you haven't been able to convince an established lecture agency to put you on their rolls, so at home you sit, declaiming to a blank television screen.

Get off your duff, already, and start your own lecture agency. It's less trouble than running around the country speaking all the time.

Write up your own pamphlet, modeling it on one you get from an established agency. "The Mississippi Valley Agency presents... Bertha Buttbotham... available for lectures..." etc.

The agency may consist of no more than a mailing address and a phone number, and many people with their own business offices will simply run their agencies out of them. They themselves are their only clients, but the pamphlet implies otherwise; this seems to be just one pamphlet in the agency's series, on one of its speakers.

You can produce a very nice pamphlet for very little money, send it out to all the groups you think might be interested in hearing you speak, and sit back and see what happens. Naturally, I am not guaranteeing that you will be deluged with responses; but if your pamphlet and your mailing list are good, you should get some replies—and even if you don't, you can impress the hell out of people with your pamphlet.

Now, suppose somebody calls your agency up and says, "Do you have anybody who can speak on the Equal Rights Amendment to our women's group?"

Don't just say no and hang up unless there's no hope in Hades you can come up with somebody. In fact, if you want to make things look

31

better to begin with, you might contact friends or acquaintances you know to be good speakers and ask them if you can include them on your list—just in case something comes up. If you really do know somebody who would be good on the ERA, or somebody who might know somebody, tell your caller, "Not on our regular list of speakers, but I do have some ideas. Let me check them out and get back to you." If you do hook something up, take 10 percent and giggle into your vest pocket.

Who knows? Before long, when someone calls your agency and asks who your speakers are, you may be able to say, "Well, we have Tom Grundy, a criminal lawyer, and Sylvia Pottedout, head of the Committee to Save Committees," and so on. As your agency gains prestige, you gain more contacts and speaking engagements for yourself. The agency really doesn't have to go this far for you to get yourself on the lecture circuit, but if it does and it's actually making money, hire somebody to run it for you. After all, how do you think the established lecture agencies got started?

# Become a Speechwriter

"Being a ghost" is not a difficult job. Yet for a skill so easily acquired, it carries an astonishing aura of intrigue and glamour. If you say you write speeches for so-and-so, people see you as a kind of Svengali putting ideas in the great person's head—when you know that actually you are more like a cosmetician having to come up, each week, with one more way of powdering the same old face.

"How on earth do you learn to write in another person's style?" people ask me. It's not nearly so tricky as it sounds. All you have to do is write conversationally, so that any speaker can adapt your words easily to his own speech patterns. Many excellent journalists fail miserably as speechwriters because in a way they have forgotten how to talk (on paper). Their speeches sound like written editorials which, when read aloud, instantly anaesthetize audiences.

All you need to ghost-write most speeches is the ability to imagine yourself in another time and place—and to be on the safe side, preferably one with established patriotic associations. Think of yourself as being with the Pilgrims at the first Thanksgiving, with nurse Clara Barton during the Civil War, or with Washington at Valley Forge.

You do not have to be an expert on political affairs. Indeed, the less you know the better, because even as a ghost writer for Congressman X or Councilwoman Y you will not be asked for position papers on energy or garbage collection. Such policy speeches are written by a special staff and reviewed carefully by the speaker and his closest political advisors.

The speeches that a ghost writes, whether he's amateur or professional, seldom make the front page of the *Times*. They appear in the back pages, the social sections, and on the front pages of local newspapers and magazines. They are the bread and butter of American oratory, written to be delivered by Governors' aides or TV stars at ground-breakings, ribbon-cuttings, and other such memorial events. Some of this deathless prose, of course, does reach the highest mouths in the land. A former LBJ speechwriter once coined a telling phrase to describe the speeches he had ghosted in the White House. "Rose Garden Rubbish," he called them. These were the talks the President gave almost every day in the Rose Garden to Gold Star mothers, 4-H Clubs, and Girl Scout troops. (Peter Benchley, the author of *Jaws,* had his start penning the same ceremonial bull.)

Suppose you learn that the Lieutenant-Governor is going to dedicate a new hospital wing in your town next month. Write her and offer to draft a speech for the occasion. You have one major advantage over the hacks already on the state payroll. You know more about the hospital than anybody up in the capital. Or try getting on the coattails of an alderman up for reelection. Suggest that his speeches do not adequately reflect the goodness you know to lie in his heart, and offer to beef them up.

Once you have written a few speeches and have had them accepted, you can begin to charge for your services. Keep a portfolio of what you write, and make it available to as many politicians as you can contact. Do not allow politics to impede your progress. As a speechwriter who has put words into the mouths of both Richard Nixon and George McGovern, I can assure you there is not a politician in the country who would allow party affiliation to prejudice him against a really good phrasemaker.

What should you say in your speeches? Well, the trick is not so much to say anything in particular as to paint verbal pictures. Abstractions like "freedom," "pollution," and "free enterprise" are just that— abstractions. They do not register on the senses because they have no visual impact. If you are talking about "freedom," describe the town's founding father fleeing Bismarck's Germany for the promise of the New World. Let "pollution" be a boy finding a bloated trout on the bank of his favorite stream. Let "free enterprise" be a car-wash chain owned by a black teenager.

At the end of a speech, give your paintings inscriptions. If your painting is of Valley Forge, with the shoeless and bleeding feet, the tiny fires, the cold, then your final inscription will dwell on courage, sacrifice, and love of country. The "painting with inscription" is the tested formula for ghosted speeches.

# Make the World's Shortest Speech

Lord Balfour, Britain's Foreign Secretary during the First World War, was once called upon to deliver a speech in Texas. But he was preceded by a long-winded toastmaster who used up all but five minutes of the distinguished speaker's time getting in plugs for his own Congressional candidacy.

When finally the toastmaster announced, "Lord Balfour will now give his address," Balfour stepped up to the podium and icily said, "I have been asked to give my address in five minutes. That I can easily do. 10 Carlton Gardens, London, England."

# Get Quoted in the Congressional Record

When I was a boy I visited a law office where a grandfatherly attorney had framed and hung on the wall behind his desk a speech he had given which had been printed in the *Congressional Record*. Visions passed through my head of Senators and Congressmen stopping in the midst of the vital affairs of the universe to read his pearls of wisdom. But in fact it is not like that at all. It is easier to appear in the *Congressional Record* than in the obituary column, provided that you have not just passed away.

All Congressmen regularly have speeches by all sorts of people on all kinds of subjects inserted into the *Record* under the heading "Extension of Remarks." If you have given any speech that does not contradict your Congressman's positions, whether it's on the State of the Union or the state of your son's Boy Scout troop, it qualifies as a record of something that happened somewhere in the country at some time. All you need do is write your Congressman a letter, enclose the speech, and request that he have it inserted into the *Record*. If you have a mailing address in his district there is every likelihood he will oblige you. It costs him nothing, and it is a simple way for him to show his constituency that he knows, and cares, what the folks back home are saying. If he is reasonably awake he will send you a copy, which you can frame for the benefit of your impressionable grandchildren.

# Out-Bureaucrat the Bureaucrats

A businessman in Idaho felt he had spent much of his working life filling out forms for various government agencies, and he was fed up with it. "Something must be done about this," he thought to himself. So the next time a government inspector, who happened to be from the Occupational Safety and Health Agency, came around to inspect his factory, he was prepared. "Here," he said, handing the inspector a weighty document. "Fill out this form."

The form was an all but endless list of questions about the inspector and his qualifications to inspect the factory, ranging from his entire educational history (what had his fourth-grade report card looked like?) to his job history (list all the jobs he'd ever had) to his personal life (marital status, family, etc.). The inspector was naturally scandalized. *He* didn't have to fill out forms!

But the businessman told him, "I've been filling out endless forms for the government all these years, and now you're going to fill out forms for me."

Subsequently this case actually was tested in court, and the businessman was upheld! So significant is this breakthrough against bureaucracy that stationery stores all over the country are carrying printed forms for you to assail your favorite bureaucrats with. So go buy yourself a packet of forms, and the next time a bureaucrat comes to bug you, why don't you try putting him through the ringer first?

# Lobby for Your Cause

Very few amateur lobbyists know how to swing the votes of legislators in their directions—and quite a few so-called professionals are in the dark about it, too. Perhaps that's because the basic rules of effective lobbying are entirely too obvious and simple, and so people feel obliged to overlook them, for their own eccentric reasons.

The first rule is—remember that the legislator's thing is, purely and simply, *getting reelected to the office he has,* or even better, *getting elected to a higher one.* This may seem a cynical view of elected officials; but on the other hand, it may be the essence of the democratic process as we know it. Unless a politician represents most of his constituency most of the time, he is not going to be elected to represent people any more.

Therefore, whether you're lobbying for the park benches to be painted or for the President to be impeached, don't go to your Congressman, Senator, or Town Councilman and say, "It should be done for the following eighteen reasons." Instead, prove to him that if he doesn't propose or vote for what you want, he will alienate his constituency, whereas if he follows your program, he will look very good. This is called the old carrot-and-stick approach—but you highlight the carrot and just let him figure the clout of your stick. You *never* harangue or threaten him directly. If you do, he senses that you'll never support him anyway, and he shouldn't waste his time on you.

Second, go to him with *concrete proposals* as to how you and your cause can make him look good. Write up a press release for him announcing that he will do whatever you want him to do, giving the reasons that will make *him* look strongest. You've done some valuable work for him! Chances are that if you've really done your homework on your particular subject, you know more about it than he ever will anyway, so also give him whatever supporting evidence he may need to defend "his" position.

Present the politician with a whole package, from public relations angles to points he can score with his colleagues. The most effective lobbying groups, from corporate representatives to consumer protection organizations, actually draft the laws they want, with the help of expert lawyers when necessary, and present them prepackaged to the legislators of their choice. A legislator cannot help concluding that lobbyists with this kind of sophistication and insight into his position could cause him a lot of grief if they wanted to.

What it all boils down to is that, as a wise wag once observed, in politics you can get things done or get the credit for doing them, but you can't do both. So feed the legislator's ego. Figure out how he can look good in the media. Suggest or supply graphics for the press that will do the job. Stage an event for him around your cause and get TV coverage for it—or have it filmed yourself and give TV stations the footage. Whatever you do, remember that it's all under the legislator's leadership, and you are behind him all the way, even though you may subtly have beaten, kicked, cajoled, and coddled him to assume his noble position.

# Use Your Personal Telephone Book like a Politician

In these days of miracle communications, one huge measure of your status is who you can get to on the telephone, and the main measure and symbol of your "telephoning power" is the state of "your book."

If you carry around a small, cheap address book, or none at all, you mark yourself as a walking power vacuum who's really out of touch. Take a tip from the example of one Democratic District Leader I know of in New York who is particularly famed for his book. It is leather-bound and divided between an appointments calendar and a directory of telephone numbers. No addresses here: if you're going to carry the numbers of five hundred people around with you, there just isn't room. The important thing with this politician is the impact of his opening up his book and thumbing through page after page of names and numbers. It is not just the density of the columns that impresses; it is the idea that since he always has his directory with him, he may actually have to call anyone in the book at any moment.

No time for writing letters these days. Everything has to be done right away, and preferably in the presence of the person the politician is doing it for. If you do it *now,* you get ten points, whether it works or not. If you do it later, you get three points if it works. So whether you're talking to this District Leader about some legislative crisis in Albany or the fact that your son can't find a summer job, his reaction very likely will be to whip the nearest phone out of its cradle like a gunfighter at high noon. Here's action for sure; and as he turns to the number of the State Assemblyman's apartment in Albany, or of the guy he knows who owns a camp in Vermont where your son might just land a spot as a counsellor, you get the feeling that all five hundred people in that book are standing just outside the door. If he can call the Assemblyman at home on a Saturday afternoon to get an instant answer for your question, obviously he can do the same kind of thing with every person on his list. So when he flips to an empty line and asks, "What's *your* number?" you are flattered.

What might not be obvious is that if this politician hadn't had the numbers of a few hundred people like you to begin with, the Assemblyman wouldn't have wanted to hear from him on a Saturday afternoon. The people in the book may vote for the Assemblyman in the next election, may work in his campaign, may chauffeur him between meetings if he's on a tight schedule. But they are the District Leader's own personal constituency, and he is really a walking communications center. In the presence of his book, politicians tremble and common folks are awed.

Well, you don't have to be a politician, even a parttime one like a District Leader, to benefit from this lesson. Just start thinking of "your book" as the portable directory of all your personal contacts.

The first step, of course, is to get such a book, and the second is to transfer all the numbers you now have and might use into it. As you do this you will be amazed at the number of people you actually know. You'll remember people you're out of touch with and see good reasons for calling them. Maybe you'll see them in combinations you hadn't thought of before. Here is an actress; there is a director. Here is a plumbing contractor; there is a friend who's about to build a new house. Here is an avid bridge player who can't find enough people to play with; there are some people with an ongoing bridge club. Remember—a successful matchmaker is never forgotten. When you get your college's alumni magazine and read your class's news, for instance, you'll ask yourself, How about some of those people? What are they doing now? Are there any you might like to renew acquaintances with? Once you start thinking along these lines, you will find yourself with a few hundred entries in your book. Now you are prepared to start building.

The next time you meet someone whose number you'd like to get, you won't fish around for that stub of a pencil you thought you had in your coat pocket and scribble his name and address down on the back of an old matchbook cover. You'll pull out your book with the pen inside and inscribe his seven digits alongside all the others. If it's someone important who has perhaps been hesitant to give you his number, he will feel better when he sees that you also have several hundred other people to deal with and won't be calling him every other day, but only if something important comes up. If it's a new social acquaintance, you will reinforce the memory or meeting him in your own mind as you enter him in your directory, and he will get the idea that you don't intend to forget about him as soon as you take your leave. And by the way, it doesn't hurt either to have a few of your personal cards tucked away in your book, just for the benefit of people who don't carry their own books around with them.

A few words about getting the numbers of important people. Obviously you don't just go up to the editor of the newspaper or the town's leading politician or socialite, whip your book open, and say, "Number, please!" You get them talking about what they are doing— writing an editorial on the pollution in your local river, sponsoring a bill to increase aid to education, planning a concert for Beethoven's birthday. Whatever it is, it sounds interesting to you, and you have quite a few friends who might be interested, too.

One invaluable tactic is to ask questions until you run up against one the person can't answer at the moment: "Most people I know think the pollution in the river comes from the chemical factory. Is that true?"

"I'm not sure yet; we're doing a study on it. I should have the results tomorrow."

"Oh, well I'd like to know, because maybe I can get a lot of friends to write letters about it, or even organize a protest around your editorial."

"Listen, why don't you give me a call in the morning?"

"Fine." You whip out your book. Maybe as you leaf through to the spot for your new entry, your eye catches the name of someone who goes boating on the river all the time. "Oh . . . this guy would be very interested. He may even have a good idea where a lot of the pollution is coming from."

You've more than made your point. The editor sees your book as a possible raft of new subscribers; the politician sees it as a possible raft of new supporters; the socialite sees it as a possible raft of new people who will buy or even push concert tickets.

You are no longer just another individual, but a spokesperson for or entree to all those personal contacts you're displaying. And if you're not hesitant about calling your boating friend up and saying, "Listen, I met the editor of the paper the other night, and I was talking to him about pollution in the river. He's doing an editorial on it. I said you might know something about it or might want to help in some way. . . ." Then he can hardly help being impressed, and you are well on your way to using and building "your book" like a real politician.

# Have the Washington Bureaucracy Eating Out of Your Hand

In the latest *Webster's Unabridged Dictionary* there is the word *grantsman*. It is defined as ". . . one who is proficient or adept in procuring a grant, appropriation or loan from a government agency." Washington is full of such types who prefer to call themselves consultants when they hire out their services.

From a veteran grantsman on the Washington scene, I learned the method to wrangle government authorization of your favorite project. It's called the "old toothpaste tube formula." You know how you squeeze out toothpaste from an old tube—you start out at the bottom with pressure from your thumb and forefinger.

Let's say you want a grant for a new sewerage facility in Podunk City.

First you go to your public library and ask for the *United States Government Manual*. Under "Health, Education and Welfare" (HEW) look for the Director of Sanitary Services. Then write him—or better, call him (his telephone number is listed)—and ask for an appointment.

The next step is the hard one, because your job is not so much to persuade him of the worthiness of your project as to relieve him of his paperwork. The one unmistakable law of Washington is, "You never sign what you write, and you never write what you sign." That means you have to prepare the thirty-seven-page recommendation for his signature. It is not so hard as it seems—it's just time consuming. If you take the Director or his secretary out for lunch, you might get your hands on an old application already filed. With the old one as a guide, fill out your own.

Once you have the recommendation ready for the Director's signature, you have pressed your forefinger on the bureaucratic side of the tube. For the thumb and political pressure, locate (in the *Congressional Directory*) a member of the House Appropriations Subcommittee on HEW. Perhaps your own Congressman can introduce you to him.

During the days you spend in Washington preparing the memorandum for the Director's signature, get to know the Congressman's staff, his Administrative Assistant (A.A.), or his secretary. Be interested in them and they will become interested in your project. Don't go buying a book for the A.A. or sending flowers to the secretary. You are not engaged in bribery; all you want is for one of them to call the Director in HEW and say, "The Congressman is deeply interested in the Podunk City project." Since the Congressman's committee is the one that funds his staff, the Director will get the message and sign his name to the already prepared recommendation. Between the bureaucratic finger and political thumb, the approval gets squeezed pretty fast through government channels.

# Be a Fourth of July Orator

A couple of years ago, my friend Don Whitehead, a government official with sub-cabinet rank, called me and said, "Jamie, I'm going back to my hometown to give a Memorial Day address. I know what to say about my work, but I have to say something that's really inspiring and I can't think of anything that hasn't been said a hundred times before. Can you come over and help me out?"

When I arrived and sat down in his office, I said, "Don, why not say something about the Declaration of Independence—you know the Bicentennial is approaching."

The idea I gave him was simple but basic. Everyone knows how the Declaration begins—but like an inscription worn smooth on old coins, the meaning has lost its edge. Read the opening words that Jefferson wrote at 6th and Market Streets in Philadelphia: "We hold these truths to

43

be self-evident, that all men are created equal, that they are endowed by their Creator with certain . . .''

Then stop and ask, ''What kind of rights were they? Was it '*in*alienable' or '*un*alienable'—most of the audience won't be sure.'' Then say, ''Well, Jefferson wrote 'inalienable'—that's the way it's written on the Jefferson Memorial. But in the actual document kept in the National Archives, the word used is 'unalienable'—the way the revision committee of Franklin and John Adams changed it.''

Does it really make a difference? Yes, all the difference in the world. You see, ''inalienable'' is a good legal term still used today to describe rights that cannot be taken away involuntarily but that may be given away *voluntarily*. On the other hand, ''unalienable'' although now an archaic word, described in the eighteenth century rights given by God that could not be given away but had to be kept in trust for one's children or one's childrens' children. Now in those two words, there is enough food for thought for a thousand words about our duty to our forefathers to preserve those basic rights for our children.

My friend Don said, ''Gee, Jamie, that's really a great concept but how would I close it? I want a real zinger.''

''Well, Don,'' I said, ''You've been at the Oval Office—did you ever see that painting of the signing of the Declaration that hangs just outside?''

''I think so,'' he replied. ''What about it?''

I explained that it was not finished because the artist who had been commissioned by Congress died. Only outlines of unsketched figures are visible in the background.

''Describe it,'' I said to my friend. ''Say that possibly there was a message—that maybe it was the plan of Divine Providence—that all of us are meant to be in that background. Elaborate. Then for the closing read the last lines of the Declaration; although they are just above the signatures, few people seem to remember them as well as the opening lines: 'And for the support of this Declaration, with a firm reliance on the protection of Divine Providence, we mutually pledge to each other our Lives, our Fortunes and our sacred Honor.' ''

Although Don did great justice to the idea, any one of you could deliver a splendid oration by taking this concept and verbal picture, reducing it to your own words, and relating it to your own experience.

# Get Elected to Congress

About twenty years ago a political science professor in Washington, D.C., assigned his honor students a curious research task. They were to survey the nation's congressional districts to see if they could come up with one that fulfilled two requirements: first, the constituency had to be marginal—neither strongly Democratic nor strongly Republican; second, local opinion had to reveal that there was at least one major issue that had not yet been exploited.

The professor's students came up with a West Virginia district whose voters were just beginning to question strip mining. The professor promptly moved to West Virginia, campaigned against the coal companies and was elected by a comfortable margin.

The moral of this story is that carpetbagging often pays. One kingdom you have conquered is worth ten that you have built. And the secret of election to Congress often has less to do with political convictions or party affiliations than with filling an available niche.

Nature abhors a vacuum. If you can spot a political vacuum early enough, you have the jump on the other guy in proving to the voters that you are the big wind to fill it. Otherwise you'll just have to go the old fashioned route of building a constituency where you are.

The West, where the population is sparse, probably still offers the greatest opportunities to the carpetbagging office-seeker. There are so many fewer minds to bend, so many fewer hands to shake. Your best bet is probably to move to a Montana or Nebraska town that's not yet on the map. Settle down for two or three years. Be friendly. Listen to people. Talk little. Gradually allow the voters to see that the moisture behind your ears has condensed and frozen to distinguished gray. Then announce your candidacy.

Don't be concerned about your lack of experience. In those districts where the story of the railsplitter becoming President still brings tears to many eyes, it can be a real advantage. Many voters, moreover, if given half a push, will jump at the chance to confuse seniority with senility. Give them that push. Remember that the most appealing candidate is still a Mr. Nice Guy with no solutions. His utterly noncommittal campaign slogan might read: "I don't know the answers but I'm going to try and find out."

Pick one issue, preferably time-tested to appeal to majority sentiments. If you milk it thoroughly, it will be enough. Democracy itself will always do in a pinch, but if you want decent variety and local color, descend to such simplicities as the mining companies, the utilities, the agribusiness brokers, the Washington bureaucracy, or the International Communist Conspiracy—just for old times' sake.

For your compaign, rent a camper. Put a sign on top that reads, "Bob Jones wants to know what *you* think." Spend three months asking questions through bullhorns and microphones. (Don't forget to visit local newspaper editors first to ensure your coverage.) Make a list of people's grievances against the governmental body you are trying to join; after six months, summarize them, systematically quoting local nobodies. Publish the results in a pamphlet. Call it *Common Sense.*

Then launch broadsides against the enemy. Remembering to keep your one issue constantly to the fore, attack the lackeys and fellow travelers who, in concert with your principal villain, are subverting the values of This Great Country of Ours.

Above all, remember that a campaign is like an anthem. You can afford six or eight stanzas, but stick to a common refrain. The stanzas may sing of taxes or inflation or open housing or strip mining or detente. But the refrain must be always the same: "Throw the rascals out!"

# Save Your Face When You've Come in Second

Suppose you've just been defeated at something, and you are in the embarrassing position of having to say something about it. Take a cue from politicians Al Smith and Morris Udall, who both used this "politician's way out": "Well, you can't be first in everything. Look at George Washington, the very father of our country. He was first in war and first in peace—but after all, he did marry a widow."

# Dodge Difficult Issues

It is not surprising that the wily Everett Dirksen, the late Senator from Illinois, is credited with articulating the perfect formula for sidestepping when somebody tries to string you up on a nasty issue. Repeal of prohibition was just such an issue for Dirksen when he was a young candidate in Illinois, and during one campaign the opposition tried to corner him on it.

"Well," he replied, "only last night, while my wife was finishing up a needlepoint of the American flag, we had a long talk about this very subject. Here's what I said to her, and I say it to you now with no hesitation or qualification: 'Some of my friends are for prohibition, and some of my friends are for repeal. I say, let the chips fall where they may—I stand by my friends.'"

47

A variation of this ploy was used by Al Smith on this same issue. When Governor Smith was asked his position on prohibition, he replied,

"If by alcohol you mean that which is the defiler of innocence, the corrupter of chastity, the scourge of disease, the ruination of the mind and the cause of unemployment and broken families, then of course I oppose it with every resource of mind and body.

"But if by alcohol you mean that spirit of fellowship; that oil of conversation which adds lilt to the lips and music to the mouth; that liquid warmth which gladdens the soul and cheers the heart; that benefit whose tax revenue has contributed countless millions into public treasuries to educate our children, to care for the blind and treat our needy elder citizens—then with all the resources of my mind and body I favor it."

# Keep Hostile Audiences from Throwing Tomatoes at You

In the early 1970s I was serving in the State Department as Director of Policy and Plans in Public Affairs. Needless to say, one of the trickiest public affairs I had to handle was trying to explain and defend President Nixon's foreign policies to college audiences. All I can really claim that aspect of my job gave me was plenty of practice in convincing hostile audiences to keep the tomatoes in their pockets. It is a matter of some pride to me that occasionally I even managed to get people rolling around in the aisles enough to lie on the bloody things. Usually I managed this with the tried-and-true combination of praising the audience for something I found we *did* agree on and a healthy dose of humor, usually at my own expense.

For instance, a typical speech might start something like this: "Ladies and gentlemen, your generation more than any other has perceived the dangers of what General Eisenhower called the military-industrial complex. While I myself have not always agreed with the specific objectives of recent student protests, I think the general principle that the military should always be subordinate to the democratically elected civil branch of our government is far more vital in the long run.

"Indeed, as students of government in the audience know, our founding fathers were well aware of the perils of an autonomous military establishment. Many of you believe that maintaining too great a defense establishment in peacetime represents a reckless flirtation with those perils. Well, it may encourage you to know that back in the days of the Constitutional Convention, Elbridge Gerry, who was later to be Vice-President under Madison, rose to address George Washington, who was presiding, on this very subject. 'Mr. President,' he said, 'a standing army is like an erect member. While it may provide excellent assurance for domestic tranquility, it often invites temptations for foreign adventure.'"

After such openings, I seldom had any real problems with the audiences. They were ready to listen to my message even if they didn't agree with it.

It is well known that the devil has no sense of humor. If you have one, therefore, you must be just another human being like everyone else. So your first objective is to show the audience that you don't have horns, and that you know *they* don't have horns—that nobody has horns.

If you can't find at least one point of agreement you can praise your hostile audience for, you can always commend them for their fairness and openness of mind. After all, they did invite you to speak. When it comes to the humor, never use canned jokes that have nothing to do with the occasion or with your subject; the audience will feel you're insulting them and mocking their concerns.

Personal anecdotes in which you make fun of yourself or your situation are often the best, if they're to the point. Even "practical jokes" can turn the trick. One government official in a situation similar to mine actually had an aide bring a case of tomatoes to one particularly touchy engagement and place it on the front edge of the stage. "I took up a collection in my office for these," he said. He continued, "We appreciate your political feelings as well as the high price of tomatoes nowadays, and we feel very strongly that the meagreness of many students' budgets should not stand in the way of their freedom of expression." Then he produced lots of little packets of salt and a pile of

49

napkins. "Of course if your principles prohibit your wasting good food on my face, we can always eat them."

Needless to say, the students were in hysterics, and when he picked up a tomato, salted it, took a bite, and strolled toward the podium, the tomatoes got eaten and he got to speak in peace.

Now, this was a particularly risky maneuver. After the event I asked this colleague what he would have done if just one student had rushed the tomato case and started firing.

"Only one way to go then," he smiled. "Take off your coat, yell 'We used to have food fights when I was in college, too!' and pitch into the battle."

Of course, once you have managed to make the audience keep its tomatoes in its pockets, you still have your own message to deliver; and in any substantial speech, you have to present your facts and argue your conclusions from them. With hostile audiences, this is best done by relying heavily on a debating technique, much used among politicians, called "cross-quotesmanship." This ploy, which is illustrated above in my quoting Eisenhower to an anti–Republican-Administration audience, involves citing conservatives as authorities for liberal or radical positions, or vice versa. Often it is used to make an opponent seem rigid, as when Senator Sam Ervin quoted Caesar Chavez and Margaret Mead in arguing against the Equal Rights Amendment. But here it serves less to make your point than to convey to the audience that a paragon of the kind of leadership they are identified with represents some vital thing you stand for.

Praise for the audience on a point of agreement, humor, and "cross-quotesmanship"—remember these threee tactics the next time you think of perhaps wearing a raincoat to a speaking engagement.

# How to Be a Clean-Sounding Dirty Politician

If you want to mention something embarrassing about an opponent but get no guff that you are playing dirty politics, do what Cicero did with Catiline, his archrival, before the Roman Senate: "I will not mention that Catiline . . ." Over and over, in saying what horrible things Catiline had done which he would not mention, he mentioned them.

Nowadays, of course, you have to be a little more subtle about such things. But Tom Dewey's insistence that the fact that Adlai Stevenson was divorced was not an issue in the 1952 campaign was a perfect example of Dewey's doing Ike's dirty work for him. A politician who says, "I don't want anyone to vote for me just because I'm Italian," turns the trick around, getting in a plug to his Italian constituency. Carter used the "Cicero Gambit" to the hilt in his presidential campaign when he announced in every speech that "Ford's pardon of Nixon is not an issue" and that he had instructed his staff not to mention it.

Of course, if you want to be really dirty, you might want to employ what is known in the trade as the "L.B.J. Gambit."

Supposedly an aide to then-Senator Johnson came to his office expressing concern about the popularity of a Johnson foe who was running for Governor.

"Spread the story," was the advice, "that as a young man he fornicated with pigs."

"But we can't say that!" the aide protested. "It's just not true!"

"I know," Johnson allegedly said. "But I'd like to see him figure out how to deny it."

# Vote on Controversial Issues

Some fifteen years ago, when I was a young and green twenty-eight-year-old legislator in the Pennsylvania General Assembly, the hottest issue going was busing to parochial schools. One day while I was musing aloud to some friends about the constitutional separation of church and state and wondering how I should vote, an old Harrisburg veteran interrupted me to introduce me to the facts of political life.

"Humes," said the sage, "there's only one way for you to decide how to vote on an issue like this. If you recall that you have a majority of Protestants in your district, and a highly vocal minority of Catholics, you can plainly see that you're going to lose no matter how you vote. *But—you'll always lose less if you vote on the losing side.* So figure out who's going to win and vote the other way."

This weird advice is golden for those occasional issues that will split you up the middle while you're trying to sit on the fence. If the question happens to be whether to tear down the old courthouse, which most see as an administrative monstrosity but many regard as a sacred architectural landmark—vote to save the old hulk. The winners won't hold it against you and will soon forget about it as they applaud the bulldozers tearing the guts out of Old Bailey. But the losers will much note and long remember the way you stood up to those philistines. They will come up to you as you stand there watching the demolition with misty-eyed reverence, clap you on the back, commiserate with you, and swear to support you in the next election.

So whether the issue is abortion or legalized bingo, building a bridge or razing a railroad station—if you don't know or don't care which way you go, as long as it's off the fence and into office again—be a loser.

# Chair Meetings like a Railroad Engineer

Formal business meetings of "democratic organizations" have the richly deserved reputation of being among humanity's most tedious wastes of time. This is because too many people, and especially people who chair these meetings, widely believe that the rules of democratic decision-making guarantee all kinds of bullies, blusterers, and other bullshitters the constitutional right to waste other people's time.

The vehicle for most meeting-persecutions is parliamentary procedures whose bible is taken to be *Robert's Rules of Order*. This venerable document hundreds of pages long may be fine for learning how things are done (or not done) in the U.S. Congress, but it is a positive menace to almost all meetings in which it is used as the final authority on "order," because it can be used to create more chaos among generally orderly people than any other volume ever compiled by mankind.

At one recent dinner where I was scheduled to speak at 8:00, the vast majority of people present (including myself) squirmed in their seats until 10:02 while a couple of clubhouse lawyers argued back and forth on one simple issue (whether the bylaws should be amended to allow associate members to vote) and indulged in ceaseless side-skirmishes on the precedence of tabling motions and moving the previous questions.

This happened for the same reason things like this always happen—because the chairman did not do his job, which is to keep the meeting on its tracks and make it run on time. Instead he looked on himself as a neutral referee whose only job was to make sure the clubhouse lawyers hogged the whole show strictly according to a set of obscure and arcane rules.

If you are elected to chair meetings, remember that most people go to meetings not in the hope of watching fights, debates, or other misplaced manifestations of people's weird egos, but in the hope of getting the necessary business done and getting out at a reasonable time. The *majority* has elected you to run that show, and that is an executive responsibility. They've picked you as the best person for the job, and if you do a good job, you will end up with the continued support and appreciation of the majority every time. This is all the advice you really need to chair a meeting like a railroad engineer. With this in mind, for every meeting you want to run with merciful efficiency, you should:

1. Prepare beforehand an agenda of what you think the meeting needs to decide (or hear about), and in what order, and send it to members with the meeting announcements. People who want other items added to the agenda may submit them in writing to you before the meeting, but usually you'll get no additions.

2. Sound out key members about what specific actions ought to be taken, and get a strong nucleus committed to particular solutions. If you can, get the actual wording of a motion people will support and line up who will offer it, who will second it, who will speak for it, and even how many will vote for it. This doesn't mean you "railroad" the meeting! It just means you do some constructive caucusing beforehand and come up with a concrete proposal for people to consider. If people object, let them do some time-saving preparation of their own; they will learn that a well-thought-out, well-written proposal has the advantage every time, especially if it's brief and simple.

3. During the meeting, rule out of order anyone who wastes time or creates diversions to deciding the items on the agenda. It is perfectly legitimate to cut off people when they speak on and on, ramble from the point, repeat themselves, insist on speaking ten times to the same issue, interrupt others, etc. Of course, you do this politely: "I'm sorry, Jack, but I'm going to have to rule you out of order. You made that point already." As long as you're evenhanded about it, Jack will say, "Oh, sorry," be embarrassed, and shut up.

4. Above all, remember that the cardinal law of *Robert's Rules* and all parliamentary procedure is that if someone objects to any ruling of the chair, it is up to him to appeal it, and then up to the majority to decide whether it wants to overturn or uphold the ruling. So, if someone doesn't like the way you're conducting a meeting, put the burden on him to interrupt things and ask whether the majority agrees with him. You will find that if you forget about *Robert's Rules* and use your common sense, precious few of your rulings will ever be overturned, and after a while even the most stubborn clubhouse lawyers will forget about *Robert's Rules* too and stick to the real issues.

A few more tips:

*Keep formal motions to a minimum.* If you let them, people will move that since there was no toilet paper in the bathroom the last time they went, the secretary should write a letter to the janitor calling him an incompetent idiot. Then you will get caught up in the parliamentary labyrinth of someone moving to amend the motion to strike "idiot" and substitute "inconsiderate individual" for "incompetent." Just say, "I don't need a formal motion on that! Somebody just write a note to the janitor! Next item!"

For less trivial cases, but ones you don't care about, such as switching the order of the agenda around—or really, anytime you can get away with it—again, say "I don't need a formal motion on that. What's the sense of the meeting? (How do most people feel about it?) Let's see a show of hands." You take a quick look, rule in favor of the majority, and say, "Okay, we'll do it that way." The "sense of the meeting" poll assures your decision of support, so nobody will challenge it; but it only takes about two seconds, and it doesn't open you up to all the flak that can erupt when a formal motion is on the floor.

And if you've prepared the ground correctly, you can often dispense even with voting on formal motions. Once it's clear to everyone that a motion is going to pass anyway, you say, "Any objections to adopting this motion?" Nine times out of ten the losers will see the handwriting on the wall and not raise objections. The motion is recorded as having passed unanimously, and you are spared the tedium of a hand-count or roll-call vote. And so is everyone else.

Finally, if you have a few members who insist on obstructing meetings with endless motions which may be in order according to *Robert's,* but which mess things up so badly that no one else can follow what's happening, you can get your organization to throw *Robert's* out entirely and adopt much-simplified rules of order based on *Robert's,* but suited to the uses of ordinary decison-making bodies. The best way to go about that is to take the scissors to *Robert's* yourself, or have a parliamentarian help you, so you end up with a version tailored to the needs of your particular organization. This is what the International Ladies' Garment Workers' Union has done. The League of Women Voters has also produced simplified rules of order. If you can get your hands on these, they should help. But beware of various rewrites of *Robert's* in your local library. Some of them are even worse than the real thing.

The strong but evenhanded meeting chairperson is one of the rarest and most highly prized birds in our society, at least among those who regularly attend meetings—and for good reason. If he falls down on the job, the whole organization is likely to collapse from boredom. But if you just remember that you can do anything if you and the majority agree, you will win the undying gratitude of those whose time and sanity you've saved.

# Make People Get Your Point

A recent study at the University of Wisconsin has shown that addressing your listener by name just before stating your point is a powerful way to help yourself be understood. If you conclude a series of remarks with, *"Tom,* the problem is *marketing* the idea"—psychologists say Tom's name will trigger an increased alertness and attention that will imprint your conclusion more deeply in his memory.

Some successful trial lawyers seem to have known about this for a long time, and I have often noticed them using the technique with juries. In the middle of his summation, the defense counsel will use the name of the foreman: "Mr. Johnson, I know you were aware that the prosecutor ignored this fact, but..." A few lawyers even memorize the names of all the jury members and intersperse them throughout their presentations. The technique works (as long as you don't overdo it to the point where people notice it as an unusual habit of yours) because a person's name is used to single him out for a personal message—to "call" him—and his reaction to it is instinctive. It says you have given him your exclusive attention, and his mind automatically reciprocates. This illustrates a more general point about making your point: always demonstrate close attentiveness to your listener, as though you were really listening to him.

If you are trying to make your point *over* someone else's in a situation like a debate, a trial, or a group discussion, your objective is just as much to keep him from getting his point across as it is to make your own. After all, if your audience doesn't get his point at all, they're only left with one option—yours.

The crudest and, therefore, perhaps most brilliant application of this strategy was employed by defense attorney Clarence Darrow. While the prosecutor was engaged in a long and crucial speech, Darrow was listening and smoking a cigar. The eyes of the jury members went to the renowned defender now and then, and after a few minutes people began to notice that he hadn't flicked the ash off his cigar; it was dangerously long, obviously about to drop off at any second.

The jurors were captivated by this mini-drama. The prosecutor argued on, and the ash on Darrow's cigar got longer: an inch and a half, two inches. The avalanche would certainly fall at any second.

By the time the prosecutor was done, nobody was listening to him at all, because the ash on Darrow's cigar was six inches long. At some point the jurors' suspense must have turned to incredulity as they began to wonder what the trick was. But even if they had guessed that Darrow had run a steel wire up the middle of the cigar, they still wouldn't have heard a word the poor prosecutor said. I saw Sir Winston Churchill use this same tactic when, during an anti-American speech by a Laborite opponent, he made a great show of unwiring his hearing aid.

If such "cheap physical stuff" doesn't appeal to you, however, you can draw your opponent off his point with such reactions as not being able to understand him, or refusing to allow him to disagree with you. For the first gambit you say something like "It's not clear to me whether you're arguing for lower taxes, for more government services, or for both at the same time; but of course *my* position has always been very clear, and it is . . ." And for the second (used especially when someone appeals to apple-pie-and-motherhood sentiments), try "You've argued very heatedly against me, but as far as I can see, you haven't said anything I disagree with! I've always said taxes can and should be lowered. You're trying to pretend I'm *against* that? The only difference between us on that issue is that *I've* got a *plan* for getting government spending under control, which is . . ." Here his point is admitted, but only as a part of your larger plan.

Both of these tactics are really variations on still another trial lawyer's tactic, which is—if the opposition makes what sounds like a telling point that you can't demolish with a brief volley of facts and conclusions, ignore it. By arguing weakly against it, you will just reinforce the listeners' idea that it's important.

Sometimes tactics like these can severely frustrate an opponent, especially one who really doesn't have much to say but wants very badly to attack you. But, if you stay calm and reasonable, *he* will lose sight of his own point and discredit himself by attacking you personally. As long as you don't *react* personally, people will remember what you *said,* but only how he *acted*.

Now that you know all about how to make people get your point, it's up to you to find a point worth making.

# Dress "Fit to Execute"

A national corporation once called in a fashion consultant to advise its executives on attire. The week before the consultant's appearance, the head of the art department, who was considered the company fashion plate, was kidded mercilessly by his colleagues. "Why did they go to the trouble of hiring an outsider? All we need is for you to take us shopping."

When the consultant arrived, the object of everyone's humor was wearing a beige two-piece Italian suit with a tapered jacket and flared trousers. His patterned silk shirt bore leather cufflinks, and his solid maroon pocket handkerchief matched his tie. To the executives' surprise, the consultant insisted that, for impressing clients and conveying the image of success, the stylish art director was the worst-dressed person in the company. He had committed the cardinal corporate sin: he had drawn attention to himself.

Whatever your personal inclinations may be, there is really only one way to dress if you want to be hired or promoted by big business. You don't need a great deal of money to dress this way, and you don't need to be aware of the latest fashion trends: indeed, too much knowledge of what Rome and Paris are up to can be a frightful drawback. All you have to remember is that an executive is expected to be ruthlessly efficient in getting the most for other people's money. He is classical and conservative, demanding the highest quality, the best longterm investment with the fewest risks, in everything, right down to his underwear. If *big* business is to believe you can handle its money with discretion, your clothing must mirror that discretion.

The standard executive uniform is a conservative three-piece pinstripe suit, a white or blue shirt, a polka-dot or regimental striped tie, black socks, and wingtips. I know one New York lawyer who survived his first struggling years on only three suits: a medium gray, a charcoal pinstripe, and a navy pinstripe. He owned one set of informal clothes: a navy blue blazer and gray slacks. For cold weather commuting he had a heavy black topcoat and a beige raincoat. (Raincoats are the one exception to the rule of somber colors—a dark slicker marks you as irretrievably lower middle class.)

The descriptions your appearance should call to mind are "cautious," "steady," "good head on his shoulders." "Sharp" is about as risqué as you should get—but no sharper than an accountant's pencil. Leave the flair to the art department.

The same advice applies to women, although there is no set uniform for them, and people would start to talk if they noticed a female executive with only three changes of clothes—which they undoubtedly would. If you are a woman hoping to (or hopping to) break into the top of the corporate structure, you cannot dress like a model. The swinging singles image is OK for the secretarial pool, but if you mean to be accepted as an equal among the moguls, you must look the part. Tailored suits and "sensible" shoes are the best investments. An occasional pantsuit or a particularly colorful scarf are permitted to break the monotony of the Brooks Brothers line, but no knee boots, please, and no jeans. I don't care if your I.Q. is twice that of Milton Friedman's; if you wear a miniskirt to the interviews you will not get the job. You may know what to do with your legs, but that's all that'll get across.

A word of consolation to those who think the rigors of such corporate dressing may cramp their style. Most of the traveling salesmen I know have taken to packing two sets of clothes: a gray pinstripe suit for calling on clients, and a leisure suit set off by pendants for the bars.

# Become a Trend-Setter in Mod Fashion

Suppose not even fifty grand a year is enough to induce you to put on a pinstripe. Your bohemian soul revolts at such conformity, and in your heart you want to look like the art director described in the previous chapter. What's more, you want to set the trends, not follow them. You are confident your psyche can take the chatter of the secretly envious, and you want to be able to page through the latest *Vogue* with a snicker, thinking, "Hell, I was wearing this stuff six months ago."

There is one simple way to ensure that in March you will be wearing what nobody else in your set will find out about until October. No, it is not to take out lifetime subscriptions to the big fashion mags—they are *always* six months behind. Innovation in fashion does not originate in Paris salons, but wells up florid and madcap from a source you would never suspect: it comes up, in short, from the streets.

That's right. Think about it. A couple of years ago it became fashionable in certain New York circles to attend fancy parties, openings, even the opera, in the regulation evening clothes—plus sneakers. An Yves St. Laurent jacket, and good old Keds down below. Only the most avant-garde of the sherry set were able to get away with this radical twist at first, but by the end of the first season it had become a trend, and old Yves himself had started thinking about designing in canvas.

And where had this mod trend begun? Why, two miles north on Park Avenue—in Harlem. Sneakers had been acceptable "formal" footwear in the ghetto years before their status drifted downtown. By the time *Newsweek* discovered sneakers were the latest fad, the black fashion setters had moved on to something else.

Or take beads and turquoise jewelry and pendants. Around 1970, when these ornaments began to seem ubiquitous in the fashion of The Establishment, the big fashion mags ran frantic articles trying to determine where the trend had begun. Some traced it to Yves' trip to Africa.

Others credited Renaissance-inspired Italians. Nobody seemed to notice that America's own hippies had been wearing beads for the past five years. By the time Leonard Bernstein got around to draping medallions over his turtlenecks, the hippie movement had moved to Pasadena and was looking for a job.

Check out magazines that are targeted to black or "youth-culture" audiences. Check out what's happening on the Country and Western circuit. Remember that the "have-nots" have one thing that the "haves" have not: style. One summer a few years ago a guy out in Topanga Canyon took a thread and needle to his old jeans, and now everybody from Forty-second Street to Hollywood Boulevard is wearing embroidered Levis. Pick up on what's going down, and you can't lose.

Be careful, however, not to copy anybody from footwear to earrings: you will just end up looking like a displaced person. Select one or two touches that turn you on, and adopt them. Make them set off your nontrendsetting wardrobe. Maybe bandanas frighten you, but gaudy pinky rings are just to your liking. Maybe nothing could compel you to wear white socks with brown loafers, but you'd jump at the chance to be the first person this side of poverty to be seen wearing an army surplus jacket to Maxim's. Select what is to your own taste, and before long you may discover that you have defined the taste of your peers.

# Go After Your Next Job

Right after the November 1976 election, there were scores of White House staffers including me facing unemployment on January 20, 1977. We sent résumés out to every conceivable contact, but after a month offers were still not even trickling in. So senior members organized a seminar, led by top New York headhunters, on the techniques of job-hunting.

First, we were told to look at the Sunday New York *Times* and the Tuesday *Wall Street Journal,* not only for leads but also for job descriptions, from which we could learn how best to package our talents. One man might call himself a Program Planner, while a colleague with identical experience would be a Research Director or Government Affairs Specialist. It was important, the headhunters advised, to use the currently marketable title.

Second, we were warned not to answer advertisements directly, but to rent a post-office box under an assumed name and have replies sent there. Once we learned the name of the hiring organization, we should try to find a friend with a job or a contact within the company. Being recommended by an employee would assure us of a much more personal interview than would be possible if we came straight from the personnel office.

In addition, we were advised to study prospective corporations through back issues of *Fortune* and *Business Week* and apply only to the companies with successful programs exactly suited to our needs and qualifications. Above all, we were told, we should display confidence and act as if we were merely "between opportunities." (One result of this admonition was that a White House aide leaked to the press the erroneous information that we were all being swamped by corporate offers.)

It is, of course, preferable to be still employed while you are looking for a new job. This provides a base of operations and gives the impression that it is you and not your employer who wants you to move on. If you are not employed, at least try to get your former employer to take your calls for a few weeks after your departure. If that's not possible, engage an answering service on your own phone for calls during working hours. Since you are presumably going to be beating the streets for interviews from nine to five, failure to engage a service could cost you an interesting lead.

In looking for a new job, start with your own Rollodex or address book. Call your friends for leads, and don't be satisfied with a vague answer, such as "I'll keep you in mind if anything comes up." Ask for specific names and for permission to use your friend's name as a reference.

Whatever your work, check the Chamber of Commerce *Guide to Local Businesses* and the Yellow Pages. When you locate a suitable company, call and find out the president's name. Then hang up. Wait an hour or so and call again, this time asking to speak to "Mr. Smith" directly. If his secretary puts you off, say you want to speak to him briefly about a matter you "think will be of great benefit to his company." When you do speak to him, ask if you might stop by for a brief interview. Once you get this far, even if he finally puts you off, he is likely to refer you to his head of personnel, and being referred to personnel by the boss is not the worst of introductions. Remember, before you go for the interview, rewrite your résumé to reflect the particular needs of the organization.

If all else fails, you can follow the lead of a recent Holy Cross graduate who was seeking a job in advertising at a time when the market was depressed and opportunities limited. He placed a copy of his résumé in each of a hundred bottles, tagged the bottles with cards saying "Help! I'm at sea!" and sent them to the heads of New York's top advertising firms. Needless to say, he got a job.

# Write an Effective Job Résumé

A college friend of mine once spent a full week constructing a résumé to present to prospective employers. He included, as I recall, everything he had ever done between the ages of ten and twenty-five: high school courses, summer jobs, hobbies, membership in college societies, even the fact that he had once placed second in a Grange spelling bee. After sending this weighty tome to about two dozen firms, he was astonished to discover that, even after a month of waiting, none of them had replied. Bewildered that his thoroughness had had such negative results, he brought the résumé to a professional résumé service to find out what he had done wrong.

They took one look at it and said, "First of all, the thing's too bloody long."

For another week the service helped him hone the monster down until they had come up with a good tight two pages. He sent the revised effort around to the same two dozen employers, and six of them asked for an interview.

The clue to an effective résumé is conciseness. No employer has the time or inclination to page through half a pound of paper to get at what he or she feels is relevant. Never let your résumé run more than two pages. Include only those facts which are salient to the particular job for which you are applying, and arrange them in a clear, easily accessible format. At the top of the first page type your name, address, phone number, age, and the name of the position for which you are applying. Then list, in a few neatly spaced categories, your past education (school names, dates of attendance, majors, and diplomas or degrees), your work experience (employer's name and address, your title, and a brief description of your duties), and any publications or speeches you may have to your credit. You should list your previous jobs starting with the most recent one and working backward, being sure to include the dates of your employment on each one.

Remember that only certain things are relevant, and that the relevance varies according to the position. A public relations firm is not interested in knowing that you loaded trucks between your junior and senior years at college. A marketing research outfit does not care about your minor in chemistry. And nobody but a philatelic mail-order house wants to hear about your vast stamp collection. Select the elements of your experience that fit the position and tailor the presentation so the employer gets the impression that Fate has been working all your life to prepare you for the opening. Do not omit any special qualifications you may have, such as proficiency in a foreign language or a working knowledge of Fortran. You may include letters of recommendation and copies of your written work if you like, although it is simpler, and just as common, to place at the end of the résumé a note announcing "References and Publications on Request."

You may, of course, do as my friend did—take your life history to a résumé service and let them construct the masterpiece for you. They will do a professional job, but they will also charge a professional's fee, and there is really little point in surrendering a large chunk of your first check when, with a little perseverance, you can do the job yourself.

# Get the Headhunters to Come After You

"The headhunters!" The cry conjures up images of hostile natives pursuing you through tropical jungles, hard after the trophy of your (later to be shrunk) skull-and-accessories.

"The headhunters are after me!" A romantic notion, as long as you can imagine that you will still be around after they catch you to enjoy the full honors of such admiring attention.

Well, in today's civilized world, you surely can. No doubt it was some clever management consultant, regularly hired by top companies to scout out and screen new executive talent, who realized how completely "executive" *he* would sound if he called his ceaseless search for prime administrative bodies "headhunting."

If you can get the headhunters to come after you, you stand a lot better chance of landing that top executive job than if you walk into a personnel office with your newspaper open to the "Help Wanted" section. And even if you like the job you've got, when it becomes known that the headhunters are after you, your chances for a raise or a promotion are hardly diminished.

Obviously, no respectable headhunter is going to yearn after your résumé if you send it to him and request that he please hunt your head. He has to "get a line" on you from someone else. So if you want to find yourself fleeing so fast from the savages of corporate slavery that only the fattest of the pack can buy you out, you have first to find out what particular headhunters you would like to be pursued by, and second, to find one prestigious business figure who is willing to point them toward you with a hearty "He went thataway!"

Check out management consultant firms. The mecca of headhunting is New York City, so bow in that direction whenever you can. These firms also offer such services as time studies and market surveys.

Once you have found out which headhunters you want to hunt you (because they specialize in your thing, are used by such and such leading companies, etc.) and the name of the head of the outfit, you get the most powerful businessman you can to recommend you. What you are really looking for is the most impressive letterhead possible. If your sponsor is a bank president, officer of a company, etc., his letterhead will carry the weight you need. And you're not asking him any big favor. Naturally, you'll draft the letter yourself; all he has to do is check it over, have his secretary sign it, slip in a copy of your résumé, and send it out with the rest of the day's mail.

Your suggested draft should be short—suitable for a one-page, double-spaced letter on business stationery. "It has recently come to my attention that James C. Humes, a lawyer with wide public experience, is now considering offers for executive positions in private business. Humes is seeking a challenging corporate job that would capitalize on his background of White House staff work and international relations. . . ."

It is not that hard to do. All you need are a few dimes to track down the tribe of headhunters you want to track you down and the signature of one leading businessman, and companies will soon be calling to interview you. Even if the headhunters have come up with someone else they consider ideal for a certain executive position, they'll always throw three or four other names in for their client company to consider. But often enough the companies will fool the talent scouts and pass the headhunter's hotshot over in favor of another candidate who's made a better impression in an interview.

# Be the Boss in Job Interviews

Whether you are interviewing someone for a job or being interviewed, it helps to know a few tricks the successful "boss" will use to try and find out what he wants to know about his prospective employee. The job applicant should use variations on these tricks to find out what he needs to know about the boss and the job.

The first and most important technique for the interviewer is: Don't Talk. An interviewer who rambles on about how his company's policy is this-and-that, how things are done in such-and-such a way, and here's what will be expected of you, and sometimes that will happen, and there's a coffee pot down the hall, isn't finding out anything. He's just on his own ego trip with a captive audience. Naturally any applicant with a brain in his head will sit there nodding agreement—until it comes time for him to do some interviewing of his own about what things *he* wants made clear. It might seem a dirty trick to usher someone into your office and then sit there like a mummy waiting for him to come out with something, and of course that's not precisely what the skillful interviewer does; but when he comes as close to it as possible without being rude, he is really asking whether the interviewee is capable of being the boss, of taking executive responsibility, and of interviewing *him*.

So if you are on the receiving end of "the silent treatment"—pop your own questions. Remember that the company *needs* to fill the job, and just as the interviewer hasn't offered it to you yet, you haven't agreed to accept it yet. You are an equal bargaining partner. You are very interested in the kind of job that's been advertised, or you wouldn't be there. But—you feel your strongest talents are so-and-so, and does the interviewer think you would really get a good chance to exercise them? How? How much freedom and real responsibility would you have? Who would you be working with or under most directly? What are those people like? The salary is a little under what you might expect to get, but are there fringe benefits to compensate? What avenues are open for rapid advancement? If they are good, you might consider it.

And so on. You ask about what *you* want to know; you don't fill the gap by rehashing or expanding on your qualifications. He has your résumé or application in front of him, and if he has any questions, let him ask them.

A corollary to the you-interview-him strategy, when it's used by the applicant, is to always know beforehand your minimal conditions for accepting the job. Never leave the interview saying, "Well, I'll have to talk it over with my wife." You should have talked it over with her already, so if necessary you can say, "Well, my wife and I talked this over a great deal, and we agreed that I really can't afford to take this job, as appealing as it is, for under $28,000." After that, you don't elaborate about how you have two kids in college, and the car just broke down, and your roof leaks, or about how you're considering another offer for $28,000, or anything. Let him make his own assumptions. *You're* not going to call *him* if you change your mind; *he's* going to call *you* if he can come up with the money or terms you want. Unless, of course, they're satisfactory to begin with. Then you just say, with no hint of eagerness *or* disappointment, "Well, the terms are satisfactory."

Job interviewers often will use a host of subtle tricks to get lines on applicants. One of my favorites is to ask what comic strips, if any, the applicant reads. I might throw in that I love the funny papers, although lots of people think they're frivolous. If the applicant says he personally doesn't care for them, doesn't have the time, or whatever—fine. But if he says he reads such-and-such a strip avidly, I ask him what happened in the last episode. If he says without hesitation that he missed it, but he'd like to know what happened because the time before it had just developed that such-and-such—fine. Unfortunately I won't be able to enlighten him, because I probably haven't read the strip myself. If he tells me what happened—fine again. But if he hesitates, gets flustered, I know he's bullshitting me—he just said he followed the strip to make me think we had something in common, because he thinks that'll help him get the job. Which it definitely won't.

There are all kinds of other questions like this which interviewers will ask—about what your hobbies are, about what kinds of things you read, and so on. Although there are some important keys to a person's nature in true answers, such as that a person who reads biographies is more likely to have high personal loyalty to his boss than someone who reads poetry or science fiction, the purpose is usually to test the applicant's frankness and self-confidence; to see whether he isn't just a little *too* willing to please (or, on the other hand, whether he really can't stand "authority" and is going to resist it all the time). When possible, as with a secretary, I will give the applicant some little sample piece of work to do, such as typing a letter with all kinds of grammatical and spelling mistakes. If she types it up copying all the mistakes—forget it. If she comes back with all the mistakes corrected—perfect. If she comes back with questions about meaning—excellent, as long as there really could have been a doubt as to what I meant. If she comes back and asks me whether "associate" isn't spelled wrong—not so good. The dictionary's time is cheaper.

The funny thing about job interviews is that there have to be *two* bosses in them, or the job is not going to get done right. If you remember that, you can be the boss in a job interview from either side of the desk.

# Get Good Letters of Recommendation

There are only two real tricks to getting good letters of recommendation: writing them yourself, and finding irrelevant fault with yourself while proving you are the perfect person to fill the particular job you want.

As to the first trick, you will blow it if you try to take a further shortcut and sign and send the letter yourself. For some reason employers are not quite as impressed when they read, "Fred D. Head is the only possible choice to be Assistant Director of Name-Dropping in your Department of Deceiving the Public. Signed, Fred D. Head," as when someone else substitutes his name for yours.

But assuming that you've got some heavy lined up to recommend you who shares your own high opinion of yourself, the only polite thing for you to do is save him the trouble of Thinking About Your Qualifications and Assessing Your Potential and Getting That Damned Letter Written One of These Days, and put the words in his typewriter. He will be pleased at your considerateness when you hand him his draft.

Now as to the second trick, which is famous enough to be known by its initials (IFF: Irrelevant Fault-Finding), you have to use a little subtlety here, too. The basic principle is that you credit yourself with attributes that make you a dynamite candidate for the job you're seeking—but since nobody is perfect, and the judgment of the person recommending you won't count for much if he doesn't show some insight into your limitations, you consign your faults to some area that would only be relevant to a job you're not seeking. A good letter of recommendation is like a masterful painting; it's the shadows that make the perspective seem real. Just make sure the shadows fall where you want them.

Let's say you're after a job in public relations. You write something like, "For creativity, ingenuity, drive, and persuasiveness, Fred has no peer." But a little farther down, do you slip in, "Of course I'd never trust him to do the laundry"? No. That's a little *too* irrelevant. Something like, "If I were looking for someone who would also be a wizard at managing the office, Fred wouldn't be the first guy I'd turn to," has a slightly better ring.

There are times when you can turn the IFF paragraph around so even it is an asset. For instance, if you are recommending yourself for admission to college but you are so shy you never go out of the house, you can say, "Elizabeth has a dignified reserve about her which invites more respect than popularity. She may never be a head cheerleader, but she certainly will be diligent in her intellectual pursuits."

This tactic is taken a step further when you get a negative recommendation from someone with "negative credibility." You usually don't go about this yourself, but it can happen on its own, as it did with me during my security check for clearance to work in the Nixon White House. The FBI contacted a law school classmate of mine, a Democrat on the left in the political spectrum. Fortunately, being aware of the IFF principle and its various corollaries, he praised me in general terms; but when pressed for anything that might evidence instability in my character, he finally allowed (not wanting to hurt me, of course, but unable to bring himself to conceal this information from the FBI), "Well, if you must know, Humes is one of those patriotic nuts who flies his flag on the Fourth of July, cries when the National Anthem is played at football games, and still thinks there's all kinds of Communist subversion going on in this country." His fault-finding somehow did not delay my rapid clearance. If he'd said, "Humes is *my* idea of the perfect patriot," I would have been forced to wring his neck. So if you're ever going to be recommended for something by someone with "negative credibility," make sure he has the good sense to attack you for all he's worth.

# Get a Day Off for Verbiage

In the English boarding school I went to in my year before college, attendance at classes was as strictly required as it is at most jobs. But one time I found myself so far behind in writing a paper that I desperately needed a whole day off to finish it. So I wrote a note to my "house mother" that I was suffering from a severe attack of ergasophobia—a recurrent condition with me, which was not at all dangerous, but resulted in listlessness, extreme fatigue, and virtual immobilization. It usually passed with a day of rest, my note said, so I would confine myself to my room, and would she please inform my teachers that I was indisposed.

She did so, and no one broke into my room to drag me off to classes. It was late afternoon, and my paper was finished, by the time she submitted my note to the school doctor, who must have smiled when he told her that *ergasophobia* means "a morbid aversion to any work."

# Get a Raise

It's gone far enough. You simply cannot wait any longer. You dread it, but it can't be avoided. It's time to ask for that raise. How do you do this without appearing the whining lackey? How do you both maintain your dignity and achieve the desired result?

The trick is to put yourself subtly on the same level with your employer. Demand an appointment immediately. If his secretary puts you off, insist that you want to see Mr. Bigg on a "very personal" matter which can't wait. (This will be perfectly true. What could be more personal to you than the size of your paycheck?)

When Mr. Bigg opens the door, say you would like some advice. "I know this may seem pretty forward of me, Mr. Bigg, but I can't help admiring how you seem to know everybody who works for you personally. You such a success and all, I mean. And I was wondering, sir, just how you saw *me* in your organization. I mean, do you think I'm making a contribution to your work here, and do you see a future for me?"

This puts the ball in Mr. Bigg's hands, forcing him to ask you how long you've been with the organization, what kind of work it is you do, and whether or not you are happy in it. This in turn gives you the opportunity to sing hymns to the department you are lucky enough to have been assigned to, to assure Mr. Bigg that you are not only very happy with your work, but you consider it a great honor to be associated with someone with such exemplary qualities of leadership, foresight, etc.

"However," you wind up your spiel, "I am getting to the age where I have to start thinking about my security. I have seven little ones at home, you know."

When he asks you what you're getting at, hint that you've had inquiries from rival firms, and that only loyalty to his fine organization, frankly, has kept you thus far from considering them more seriously. "If I could be assured, sir, that I would be in for some more responsibility, some possibility of advancement, in the next few years, why then . . ."

This tack is much more likely to get you the raise than a straight-out request. Executives distrust directness; they think it conceals something under the surface. Deviousness, on the other hand, is their meat and potatoes. So if you want a raise, you don't have to ask for it. Just ask him for advice and he will suggest a raise for you.

# Get a Good Credit Rating for Next to Nothing

Many people get mildly irritated when they discover that if they disdain using credit cards, borrowing money, and generally paying interest to financial institutions in favor of paying for everything in cash, they can get to be forty years old and have no better credit rating than Woody Guthrie had when he stuck his paintbrushes in his pants and hitch-hiked out of the Dust Bowl. It seems like extortion, "You get indebted to us and pay us interest, or when the time comes for you to borrow $10,000 to open your new business, believe me, our desert will be hot and our mountain will be cold."

But actually, there is a way around this dilemma. Take the example of a distant acquaintance of mine, let's call him Jack, who happened to know a thing or two about how "the system" works.

When Jack was in college, he took a few minutes out one day to stop by his bank and borrow $1,000. He told the loan officer he needed the money to buy a car from a friend so he could take a particular summer job, which would more than pay for the car, so he'd only need the loan for ninety days. "7 ¾ percent annual rate," the loan officer said; and Jack replied, "Fine." But when he got out of the bank with the money, he decided maybe he didn't need the car after all. So, being a prudent man, he stopped by the nearest Savings and Loan Association and dropped the $1,000 in a 5 ¾ percent account. Three months later he withdrew the $1,000-plus-interest, went back across town, and repaid his loan right on time. For a quarter of a year, the loss he sustained—the difference between the two interest rates—came to five dollars.

The next fall Jack borrowed $2,500, telling the loan officer that he wanted to buy furniture for his college room which would be suitable for his first apartment after he graduated. No problem—he was already a good risk. But once more, when he thought about it, he decided maybe he'd wait on the furniture—so back he went to the trusty Savings and Loan again, and forth with the repayment three months later, taking a loss of about $12.50.

Then, around graduation time, he borrowed $2,500 for six months. By this time he didn't have to explain what he was going to do with the money: "personal business" was sufficient. Of course a couple of flourishes on the theme helped: he kept his checking account in the bank clean of any embarrassing bounces; and he maintained a small savings account, to which he added five or ten dollars every month or two, and from which he never made a withdrawal.

After he paid this $2,500 back, at a loss of something like twenty-five dollars, he waited thirty days, then borrowed $10,000 for three months. Four times the money for half the time cut into him for around fifty dollars, but by this time he'd generated more personal credit power than most people accumulate in a lifetime. Unsecured personal notes at a bank are not only the cheapest form of borrowing, they also count more than anything else toward getting a *real* credit rating, which reflects not just that you are an honest slob who pays his bills on time, but that you should be lent large sums of money of your own say-so.

Six months later Jack was laboring away in a quite respectable job with a brokerage firm when he noticed that government bonds were at an unusually high premium, and that in fact if he bought Treasury bills that were due in two months, he could get a return higher than what the bank would charge him for a loan. So he borrowed $25,000 for sixty days, repaid it right on time, and actually made money on the deal.

At this point he applied for all the major credit cards, and naturally he got them. He used them now and again, always paying off the statements in full immediately so he wasn't charged any interest. For the purposes of his credit rating, however, he could just as well have dropped them in a drawer and forgotten about them (which is another minor trick to getting a good credit rating: when the credit card company is asked how you stand with them, all they do is check whether you've ever missed payments, whether you've got an outstanding balance, etc.; they don't know you've never used the silly card, so you get the best possible rating).

Now, what happened next was that Jack got wind of a fantastic opportunity; the kind of "sure thing" that only comes to people who can swing large amounts of money around. He borrowed $300,000 for ninety days to take advantage of it. Naturally, at this point he had to explain that the loan was for a very specific business purpose, which he outlined in detail in a very carefully written loan proposal. But the bottom line was that, for total "losses" of less than one hundred dollars, he had a credit rating that not too many other twenty-five-year-olds could match. Obviously, this story could go on forever, but, so as not to turn you funny shades of green, I will refrain from telling you what Jack did after he repaid the $300,000.

# Win Fame as a Raconteur

No, a raconteur is not a restaurateur who happens to be a raccoon—no more than an anecdote is what you take to counteract the effects of poison. If you already know that a raconteur is an expert teller of little tales, of anecdotes, don't be so proud of yourself. Real raconteurs are rarer than raccoons who own restaurants, and even if you tell stories all the time, chances are that you aren't one. Unless you cut into a conversation at just the right time with your ditty, trim its sails perfectly to the winds of the occasion, build it up to just the right height of suspense, and then puncture it with its punch line in such a way as to send your audience sprawling all over the floor, you are probably just another one of those guys who tries to be funny all the time. But since you tell stories instead of jokes, you take a little more time about it than most.

A raconteur gone awry can bore more people in less time than the sound of blank recording tape. But if you persist in giving this high art the old college try, and if you can perfect it, you of course will be the delight of the cocktail party class or the lecture circuit. So here's how you might go about it.

First, if you are going to tell stories, it stands to reason that you have to have some stories to tell. These you can get from anywhere. Just don't try to tell them to the people who told them to you. Whenever you hear a really good story (even if the teller has messed it up), write it down in a kind of shorthand:

1. Japanese naval victory over Russians, 1904
2. U.S. Secretary of State William Jennings Bryan, teetotaler, at formal dinner in Japan to celebrate
3. Japanese insulted when he toasts the victory with a glass of water; start to walk out

Ambassador: THE JAPANESE NAVY HAS WON A GREAT VICTORY IN WATER, SO I TOAST THEM IN WATER. WHEN THEY WIN A GREAT VICTORY IN WINE, I WILL TOAST THEM IN WINE.
(Japanese laugh; the day is saved.)

You put the punchline in big block letters, so in case you ever need to use the story in a public situation such as a speech, you can read it off easily. As you start to collect your stories, you periodically go through them, setting aside the weaker ones and getting a "hard core" of a few dozen with a good variety of subjects, lengths, "morals," etc. Actually, all of a raconteur's repertoire is not going to be humor. Any interesting little story with a sharp, surprising, or revealing point is fair game, as long as it has quintessential entertainment value. The anecdote about "How to Get a High Credit Rating for Next to Nothing" contained in this book is an example of a raconteur's story you'd throw into a conversation about credit.

However, once you've got your sheaf of select note cards neatly numbered 1–24, 1–36, or whatever, your troubles have just begun. Remember the story about the guys who'd been in jail so long that they knew all of each other's jokes, and to save the time it took to tell them they numbered them all and just laughed hysterically when someone cried out, "17!" or "31!" or "4!"? A new guy got chucked into the slammer with them, and he thought they'd all gone mad until someone let him in on the secret. Proud to be initiated into such an "in-group" mystery, he shouted, "26!" but was rewarded with stony silence. "17!" he cried—but again, nothing. "What's the matter with you guys?'' he exclaimed. ''When the other guy said '17' a few minutes ago, you all laughed like crazy!''

''Well,'' came back the reply, ''I guess some people just don't know how to tell a joke.''

There it is. Now that you've got your stories, you've got to know how to tell them.

One of the prime tricks of the raconteur's trade is the use of concreteness and detail to make the story believable. You don't start out with ''There were these three salesmen...'' For a joke, maybe, but not for a story. If it's a historical story, make sure you have the names, dates, and background: ''Back in 1968, when student antiwar protests were just reaching their height, a friend of mine named Tom Gonzalez...''

Wherever you can get away with it, use a little ''poetic license'' to bring the story closer to your personal experience. If you can, make yourself the butt; pretend it happened to you. Otherwise, you saw it personally, or some friend of yours was there.

The addition of very specific details is the greatest aid, however, to making stories believable—as eighteenth-century playwright Richard Sheridan hilariously illustrated in *School for Scandal*. In spreading a totally false story that Sir Peter Teazle has been wounded in a duel with Charles Surface, Sir Benjamin Backbite argues that the duel was fought with swords, while Crabtree opts for pistols. Crabtree captures the belief of the company by assuring them that ''Sir Peter forced Charles to take [a pistol] and they fired, it seems, pretty nearly together. Charles's ball took place, and lodged in the thorax. Sir Peter's missed; but, what is very extraordinary, the ball grazed against a little bronze Shakespeare that stood over the chimney, flew off through the window, at right angles, and wounded the postman, who had just come to the door with a double letter from Northamptonshire.'' In the face of such detail, Sir Benjamin can only reply, ''I heard nothing of all this!'' and ''I must own, ladies, my uncle's account is more circumstantial, though I believe mine is the true one.'' But in story telling, it's not truth that makes believability, anyhow; it's detail.

Finally, your delivery. There is only one hint for this, which is that a raconteur is not a flashy, prepossessing standup comedian. He's not the slickest, just the funniest, and he is best off playing the ''poor country boy''—letting the good story he heard tell itself. Everybody knows that in a lifetime a raconteur might make up and perfect perhaps half a dozen of his own original stories that are really top-notch, and most do not even bother to try. As Lincoln, himself a famous raconteur, once said, "I'm no comedian. I'm just a retailer." So don't pretend you're not stealing your stories. Just offer them up for the company to enjoy as the classics they are.

Beyond the above hints, the secret of being a famous raconteur is the same as the secret of most of life's successes, which is practice. You wouldn't expect to be able to relieve Tom Seaver in the seventh if you'd never pitched major-league ball; but since opening your mouth is much easier than throwing a baseball accurately (not to mention fast), people by the thousands tend to think that if they tell a few of Sam Ervin's stories, they can rival one of the world's most famous raconteurs. Hardly surprising that Sam's gems often fall like leadpipe clunkers from their lips. Telling a good story well is really a lot like throwing a good strike. You have your target (your audience's collective amusement); you signal (your opening line, which responds to some theme in the conversation and announces that you're going to tell a story, but *without* saying, "Hey, I've got this really great story!"); your windup (in which you pile on the details and build the suspense); and finally, your delivery (the punchline).

If your pearl of wit is going to hit right on the tip of your listener's funnybone, you've got to perfect your timing and inflection for every story until they're completely natural. You help yourself when you thumb through your files of "active" stories and retell them to yourself, watch your audiences carefully every time you spring one, be careful to add or cut details according to whether your preparation for the punchline is racing or dragging, and notice which styles of delivery get the biggest laughs or most impressed reactions. If you tell a story you really love a few times and it draws long yawns or puzzled glances no matter how you try to vary its delivery, relegate it to your "inactive" file and bring up another one from the minor leagues. You don't have to lose it completely. You can always think to yourself, "Good old number 13," and chuckle inside.

Before you spring any story on a large audience, be sure you've tested it out first. A new story should be tried on one other person, or maybe two—preferably friends who will have a little patience if they don't find it totally hilarious and completely charming. If it gets a green light there, try it at a dinner or a party. Only when you've really proved your ability to handle the story should you slip it into a speech, talk show interview, or whatever. And remember that in a speech the prime use of the raconteur's material is to soften the audience up with a laugh and, at the same time, to illustrate or lead into a substantial point he wants to make.

# Make Funny Toasts

There was one item that Noel Coward would never travel without. It was not his toiletry kit or a favorite lounging robe. It was his rhyming dictionary.

Although it may seem incredible that such a master of lyrics and light verse would need a word prop, actually it would be incredible if he didn't. For anyone whose business is words, a rhyming dictionary is an indispensable companion. A White House speechwriter is never without one. The prop is essential because songsmiths and wordsmiths are expected to be able to come up with gems of rapier wit, often at a moment's notice, at every wedding and bar mitzvah they attend.

You really need no special talent to write light verse for these occasions. Often the worst doggerel gets the biggest laugh. In 1971 my cousin John Humes celebrated his fiftieth birthday at the American Embassy residence in Vienna. With the help of the rhyming section in the back of a *Webster's Dictionary,* I composed a ditty for the occasion on the flight over. I wrote it down on the air sickness bag. Since he had the unusual distinction of having been born in the Plaza Hotel in New York, I began:

> 'Twas the Plaza Hotel, in July '21,
> The tale of our Johnny was begun.

I admit this is not exactly Robert Frost. But it made a hit. The distinguished guests were treated to readings of birthday telegrams from Presidents and Prime Ministers, but my toast was what they remembered.

Now, I don't say that your literary efforts on behalf of this or that honored guest will put you in line for a Pulitzer. But the moral of the tale is clear:

> When you're asked to be amusing
> And you haven't got the time.
> Never underestimate
> The power of a rhyme.

# Be Introduced as a Speaker the Way You Want

Once in the 1930s Wiley Post, the famous aviator, was guest speaker at a dinner in a midwestern city. The Mayor gave an effusive introduction, closing a lengthy buildup by announcing, "Our speaker, in his world-renowned accomplishments, has transcended the courage of a Columbus, surpassed the daring of a Drake, outstripped the valor of a Verrazano and the mettle of a Magellan. Ladies and gentlemen, I give you . . . I give you none other than . . ."

He stopped, flustered, and leaning over to Post, he asked, "What's your name?" Upon learning it, he boomed out, "Wiley Post!"

So when Post got up to speak, he began: "Ladies and gentlemen, I have travelled in many places and visited many cities. But today I have experienced something more than the lure of London. I have sensed something more than the vivacity of Vienna. I have witnessed something more than the majesty of Madrid or the beauty of Budapest. For nothing in my travels has quite equalled the charm and loveliness of your own city of . . ."

Then he leaned over to the Mayor and asked in a loud stage whisper, "Say, what's the name of this burg?"

That is the kind of revenge every badly introduced speaker would cherish. Most introducers do, of course, remember your name. Sadly, that is not all they remember. In their zeal to build you up as a cross between Demosthenes and Alexander the Great, all they succeed in doing is transforming your life into a row of dull statistics. The least imaginative among them merely intone the whole dreary litany of birth date, degrees, titles, and family particulars. Since nearly all speakers have some sort of education, family, and job, the introduction cannot help but bore the audience to distraction. And no speaker wants a distracted audience.

A good introduction is like a frame for a portrait. In my experience there is only one way to be sure that the frame does not obscure the picture, and that is to make it yourself. That's right. Write your own introduction and send it beforehand to the introducer with a note running something like this: "Rather than enclosing my résumé, I am sending you a copy of an introduction that was delivered recently." Keep the copy brief, unflowered, to the point, and if you can, throw in a good anecdote about yourself—one that shows you as the butt of the humor in connection with your very impressive position. Don't worry too much about offending the Lion's Club secretary who may be staying up nights for weeks on end preparing copy of his own. You'd be surprised how many potential introducers are delighted to get rid of the job.

# Save Your Face When the Speaker Has Put You to Sleep

One time when my brother Graham was in college he was called upon to introduce Paul Tillich, the venerable theologian, to a large convocation, and to make a few remarks summarizing the great man's address afterward. Unfortunately he had been up for forty-eight straight hours finishing a couple of term papers when he stepped to the podium; so after he made the introduction, he retired to his seat just behind the great man and promptly was lulled to sleep by rolling phrases and high abstrac-

81

tions. Tillich, of course, could not see him, but the rest of the college could.

He was finally awakened by the applause following the conclusion of Tillich's address. The embarrassment of the entire community hung in the balance as he blinked his way forward to summarize a speech he hadn't heard.

"Ladies and Gentlemen," he said. "I have never been so transported by a speech in my entire life. Dr. Tillich's words carried me, as I am sure they carried many of you, beyond the realms of mere fact and logic, beyond the systems of philosophy and theology, into a virtual trance of meditation upon the presence of the Almighty. To analyze and summarize his thoughts, I am sure you all agree, would only break the spell he has cast on us. One single word is sufficient for my part: Amen."

It was only the decorum of the audience that suppressed hysterical laughter and kept my brother from getting more applause than Tillich had received.

# Get Free Research

Suppose that in a rash moment you have just agreed to address your local gardening society on the history of grafting, or that you're a college student halfway through the term with three big papers looming ahead and no hope in Hades of getting the necessary reading done in time.

There is an alternative to throwing in the towel. Write your Congressman. He or she has access to the excellent research staff of one of the world's finest libraries, Washington's Library of Congress. This staff of professional researchers spends the bulk of its time tracking down background information for government uses from policy making to speechwriting. A Congressman's request for the latest dope on Kansas wheat production or Daytona's transportation problems is all that is needed to get the best bibliographical minds in the business turned up full tilt; and if your Representative is eager to please his constituents, he will be only too glad to submit your request on his stationery. My victory in a school debating championship some years ago resulted largely from the thoroughness with which the Congress's librarians had researched my topic for me.

Do not expect the staff to write a paper or a speech for you. What they will probably send you is a brief bibliography and copies of or excerpts from relevant literature. In other words, they will take care of all that annoying legwork that so often bogs down the beginning of a project. Allow at least six weeks for delivery, and don't forget to thank your Congressman.

# Have a Title of Your Very Own

A friend of mine once ran for the Virginia State Senate. He and I both thought it was a good idea because he is tall, well groomed, and looks a bit like Abraham Lincoln. Besides, he was unemployed at the time and had no other interesting prospects. The campaign went well, but at his first rally, after delivering an eloquent speech, he was nearly stymied by a woman who wanted to know the candidate's current occupation. My friend did some fast thinking and replied smoothly, "Ma'am, I'm a free-lance writer and public relations consultant."

It was as good a title as any, and not really untruthful. Almost all of us are free-lance writers—the fact that we haven't had anything published lately hardly disqualifies us from using the title. And anyone who has ever written a press release for her niece's engagement party, or commented at a cocktail party about a TV commercial, may be forgiven for referring to herself as a PR consultant.

We all love titles. I know a lawyer who went on the bench for a few months just so he could be called "Judge" the rest of his life. If his best friend calls, his wife will announce that "the Judge is sleeping" or "the Judge is in the john." Even his own brother calls him Judge.

My own secretary, when she wants to reserve a hotel room at the last minute, calls in the name of Ambassador Humes—a nod of convenience to a three-year UNESCO commission I once served. Unfortunately, however, she doesn't always tell me she's done this, so when I arrive and the desk clerk calls me "Mr. Ambassador," I sometimes say, "Oh no"—thinking that he has me confused with my cousin John, who really *is* an Ambassador. None of which really matters. I've got the room.

If you travel abroad on business, you'll feel almost naked without business cards that supply not only your name, but also a title. In Asia and Europe, where democracy has not yet spread so thin as to make all titles as suspicious-sounding as "Baronet of Malmsey," business people would not think of having cards printed with their names alone; the exchange of titles, however spurious, is as much a part of introductions as the handshake.

There is no reason why Americans should be shy of putting themselves forward in this area. Now that masseuses are passing out cards labelled Therapist there is little excuse for inhibition. If you handle apartments, call yourself a real estate broker. If you advise students, you are a vocational guidance counselor. If you once lectured to your club on soufflés, why not think of becoming a culinary consultant? Even if you spend most of your spare time rearranging the furniture, you can pass yourself off as a home coordinator or interior designer.

By all means buy business cards. The title should be centered, in somewhat smaller letters, directly under your name. If the above examples have not sufficiently jogged your imagination, remember that whatever you do in private business, you can always present yourself as a sales representative or marketing consultant; the phrases are general enough to include any kind of buying and selling at all, even your weekly trip to the cheese store. If you are retired, you have special qualifications—whatever your experience—as a business consultant.

And as a last resort, don't forget those old standbys, "free-lance writer" and "public relations consultant."

# Join an Exclusive Club

Some years ago, a Harvard student being considered for the prestigious Porcellian Club was invited over for the evening. An entourage of officers showing the prospective member through the rooms paused before a piano in the parlor, and the president, recalling that the lad played, asked him if he would entertain the company.

"No," the young man demurred. "Please," said the older student. "Not right now," was the reply. "Oh, go ahead and sit down," insisted the officer. So the young man did. He played one tune and, when this was received with warm applause, tried another. He ended up entertaining the officers—to their apparent delight—for over half an hour.

But he never got a bid.

The anecdote suggests the secret of qualifying for an exclusive club. In fact the student's initial reluctance to play, had he stayed with it, would have served him far better than his surrender to the applause, for clubs like the Porcellian place a high premium on well-bred inconspicuousness. If enough members know you long enough, you will inevitably arouse someone's hostility. An amiable nobody with agreeable manners and a tasteful appearance has a much better shot at membership than a fast-talking, flashy dresser with confident, boastful ways.

I am speaking, of course, of the truly exclusive places, not the thousands of local country clubs that have arisen in recent years to cater to the suburban bourgeoisie. Almost anyone with the proper bank account and skin color can join one of those. I mean the established bases of *noblesse oblige*—those dimly lit rooms without signs, or those golf courses where the money is very old and very quiet, and where your fellow members are less likely to be wealthy contractors than Assistant Secretaries of State.

Since nobody within such hallowed walls is impressed by *mere* money, you should at all costs avoid appearing like a climber. The Establishment antennae are forever up to search and destroy the *nouveau riche*. On the other hand, many established clubs are habitually

85

short of money, which means they are always looking—even if they do not appear to be looking—for new members. Therefore, your chances of breaking into the town's upper crust are far from hopeless.

Timing is very important. Make a move to join when you are young or have just moved to town—before you have made local enemies by besting old timers in business deals, giving better parties, or whatever. Get to know someone who you know is a member. Work on school or business connections. Eventually you will find a member, preferably a very prestigious one, to sponsor you. Then, at the exploratory meeting, keep a low profile and avoid overt attempts to impress your hosts. *You* are supposed to be impressed by *them*. Let them do most of the talking, and try to suggest your attentive interest without betraying your eagerness to join. You cannot be rejected for what you do not say.

# Vary Your Social Fare

Have you had it with the old rounds of dinner, dancing, and Drambuie? Are you up to here with movies and plays? Do you cringe at the thought of one more Embassy reception?

Do not despair. All is not lost. All you need to pull yourself out of this morass of normality is a few stamped envelopes, the Yellow Pages, and a pen.

Do what a San Francisco friend of mine did. She turned to the Yellow Pages and then wrote to all the private art galleries in town, asking to be put on their mailing lists and advised in advance of special showings. As an unofficial member of five galleries, she was soon being invited to dozens of cocktail parties and white-wine fetes honoring artists. And, since the invitations always included two tickets, she was able to invite friends to these elegant, unusual affairs.

A slightly racier crowd may be found frequenting automobile shows. Write the major auto agencies saying you are a motor critic and would like to be advised of coming events.

If you are anxious to mix with the rich eligibles, however, nothing beats a boat show. Usually, these are held in the spring, and if they are not public, you can generally wangle an invitation by becoming friendly with a local boating and marine supply merchant. Often people in the trade receive complimentary tickets to gala special affairs, and any such merchant worth his salt will offer to take you along as his guest once you tell him you are in the market for a yacht. The real possibility, however, is that once at the boat show—however you get there—you will meet someone who is just dying to take you for a cruise in the yacht he is about to buy. Or if it just can't wait, the one he's about to trade in.

A taste for money, however, is of course not an absolute prerequisite for a more varied social schedule, and you may find yourself drawn less toward such commercial events than toward headier, more exotic fare. In that case you might join the local museums and ask to be apprised of lecture series, private tours, and exhibitions. Museums serve nearly as much wine and cheese as art galleries and, in addition, they afford you the opportunity to mix with the truly rare birds of this world. If you are lucky you may find yourself some evening chatting with an up-and-coming anthropologist about the latest Pleistocene digs.

Which beats hell out of the movies.

# Plan an Elegant Public Party

Suppose the big account from Cleveland has just blown into town. Contract renewal time is up, and you want something that will let him know in no uncertain terms that he is not dealing with pikers. How about a dinner party in his honor, but one with a special twist? He's already been to every French restaurant in town, and you took him to the club last time around. If you're going to be writing this off on the company or are filthy rich on your own, a little extra expense is only a minor problem. So why not investigate the possibility of holding the affair somewhere that is not normally used for such occasions—a place that will both charm and impress your client.

Many of the country's historic old homes, especially those run by state historical societies with chronic deficit budgets, would be delighted to open their doors to a fete honoring a modern-day captain of industry for the price of a decent donation. Have the waiters dressed in frock coats and periwigs.

Or you might charter a yacht. If some wealthy socialites have a yacht with a crew that's sitting around in the harbor doing nothing half the time, ask if you can charter it for a party for your mogul—you can even invite the owners if it's appropriate.

If you can possibly secure the use of an antique railroad car—there are a few of these elegant artifacts scattered on sidings throughout the country—it will be well worth the effort. Imagine the thrill of being thrown a party in J. P. Morgan's private dining car. The awe of history alone would assure you a lifetime contract.

The most imaginative setting for a party I have ever encountered was the tarmac of a private airfield, one corner of which a diplomat had commandeered for the afternoon to send off a visiting statesman from Burma. Drinks and dinner were served al fresco under a huge canopy supported on one end by circus tent poles and on the other by the wing of the statesman's jet.

Another kind of party, of course, can be arranged inside a plane, if you can charter a suitable one. For an all-day affair, try a morning swim in San Diego, an airborne brunch, sherry in San Francisco, topped off with a super supper in Seattle.

There is also the possibility of "outing affairs." Here you might want to take a tip from William Randolph Hearst. My friend Charles Foster Kane has told me that the great newspaperman used to trundle off periodically to the hills or beach, bringing with him an entire household staff, dozens of guests, and enough caviar and chilled champagne to keep the whole lot drunk for a week. They would camp in large, well-appointed tents miles from the bustle of the city, while liveried servants kept the chamber pots empty and Hearst discussed wagers and deals. And what more picturesque tableau could you imagine that the shaking of corporate hands beneath the swaying of the pines?

# Go to a Masquerade Party

In October 1934 my parents were invited to a Halloween masquerade party. My mother, who loved parties, was at first reluctant to go because she was over eight months pregnant. But at the last minute she decided to attend. After all, the host of the party, Dr. Nutt, was her obstetrician. Because of her protruding shape, mother was at first at a loss as to how she should go, but then she looked at the pancake-mix box and decided to go as Aunt Jemima. It was easy—just brown paint, a long skirt, some stuffing for the blouse to balance the tummy (mother was born with a figure to match the flapper age she matured in). Daddy went as an Indian chief with lots of red warpaint on the face, a headband with feathers (cardboard feathers mother had cut out and stuck into a headband), and two hand towels that were pinned to the front and back of his jockey shorts.

When they arrived at the hosts' door, Dr. Nutt, dressed as a Cheshire cat, greeted Aunt Jemima and her Indian escort. Mother said, "Doctor, I feel some twinges." "Elenor," replied Dr. Nutt, "don't you ruin my party—it's the first I've had in a year." But a couple of hours later—right when festivities were in full swing—mother sought out the Cheshire-cat host and argued, "Doctor, it's a hurry call—it's coming fast." So off went the Cheshire cat with Aunt Jemima in one car with the Indian chief following in hot pursuit. They never quite made it. My mother and Dr. Nutt got to the hospital, but I made my first appearance in its elevator at 11:55 Halloween night with my mother still painted as Aunt Jemima and Dr. Nutt still in his cat uniform.

Well, for a party my parents never expected to attend, they ended up being the central attraction. Actually, masquerade parties are often like that. Last-minute costume concoctions, like last-minute parties, turn out better than elaborately planned ones. Of course, you don't have to go through the trouble of having a baby, but you also don't have to go through the trouble of ordering in advance—an expensive costume. The makeshift Statue of Liberty costume always wins more points than the elaborate Marie Antoinette. All you need to be the Statue of Liberty is a sheet and an electric flashlight for your torch.

The sheet is a wonderful basic material for masquerades. Add a wreath and grapes and you are Nero in a toga. Pin on a halo and you are Joseph of Nazareth, or paint the sheet in many stripes and you are Joseph, advisor to the Egyptian Pharaoh. My daughter, Mary, once took a pillow-case sheet and painted on a Raggedy Ann face with slits for eyes and went trick-or-treating as the popular doll.

In just her few years of Halloweening, Mary has come up with a lot of good ideas using around-the-house items. Wearing a raincoat with a paper hat can make you a fire chief, but add a Teddy Bear and you become Christopher Robin. Using mother's panty hose, she devised such creations as Superman by adding a cape and painting a crest on her T-shirt; or she painted the panty hose green and stuck her head through a pillow case, also painted green, to become Peter Pan.

So for the next masquerade party, show you have real style by making your own. You'll save money and have more fun.

# Give a Surprise Party

An employer of mine wanted to give a surprise party for his wife. He was leaving a job in a town where they had made many friends over the years, for a different endeavor in a new community. What he had to do was get his wife out of the house on some pretext so the guests could come in and the party be prepared. Unless the excuse was logical, his wife would see through it.

My boss had a photographer friend who had taken lots of pictures of them and their family during the last few years. So it was natural that they be invited to his home for their last evening in town to look at albums and reminisce.

At the husband's insistence, they made it an early evening and returned back to the house. When they got out of the car and walked up the driveway, the wife heard music playing in the front hall. To his wife's question, my old boss replied, "I just wanted to have one last dance in the House." So to the strains of "Those Were the Days" played by the U.S. Marine Corps Band, Betty and Jerry Ford had a last dance in the foyer of the White House as a hundred of their dearest friends poured out of the State Dining Room to celebrate their last night in Washington.

As Jerry Ford knew, the secret of such a party is a combination of both surprise and nostalgia. A surprise involves an *un*usual happening within the framework of the *usual* routine. An acquaintance of mine, on his wife's fortieth birthday, had his mother-in-law suggest a shopping expedition as a special present. Meanwhile, he had the Beef and Brew House, where he usually stopped on his way home, come into their home and cater a surprise party for a hundred of her friends.

For nostalgia I knew one lady who chartered an old train to take a group of her father's friends back to the small town from which he came. The wife of a state Senator dressed herself up as an emcee and staged a "This Is Your Life" in a local hotel with the usual old school-teacher as well as the first boss. Still another friend had six-foot blow-ups made of every stage in her father's life, including cradle and choir-boy shots. Whatever you do, plan the right scenario for surprise and evoke old memories for nostalgia.

# Go Back "a Success" to Your School Reunion

Reunions can be surprising. Don't expect to see the class president or star halfback coming back in hopes of reliving former glories. Big men on campus seldom return to the scenes of their successes unless they have made it equally big in the world beyond the school walls. If the Superjock and the Head Twirler do show up, it will probably be because he's now a city councilman eager to shake hands as frequently as possible, and she's head of the alumni relations board.

Who does come back? Generally, it's the ones whose names you never could remember, even when they were classmates. The guy with the ducktail and no forehead, the girl who never dated. The ones everybody had picked as losers. My advice is be careful about rushing up to these folks and bragging about your hardware store, because it's quite likely that he's now president of XYZ International and she's a producer of the *Today* show. Nobodies in high school and college come to reunions to demonstrate that they are now somebodies. Except for a few early divorcées who have come to show off a new, unfaded mate, few real losers show up at these things.

So if you plan to return to the golden days of your youth, go on a diet early and order a tailor-made suit. When you get there, have ready a selection of falsely modest replies to give to the inevitable question, What are you doing now? If you're an ambulance-chasing attorney in a small city, you smile as though you really didn't want to pull your rank and say, "Oh, I'm just a country lawyer." A stockbroker might say, "I fool around in the market"—so if you say it, you'll be mistaken for a stockbroker. A modest super-salesman of computers can easily get away with calling himself a "peddler." The point is that your former classmates, who are probably every bit as nervous and disoriented as you are, will supply their own delusions of your grandeur; whereas if you pounce on them proclaiming what a fine fat fellow you are, they'll very likely spot you as a fraud.

One down-and-out writer I know decided he'd go whole hog to be a success as his Princeton reunion. With his next-to-last three hundred dollars he hired for the day a chauffeured limousine and a gorgeous, intelligent blonde from an escort service. In preparation, he asked me to get hold of a few dozen business cards—it didn't matter whose—from the Iranian Embassy. When old friends, naturally overawed by the blonde and the limousine, asked him what he was doing, he'd hand them the Arabic-alphabet cards, apologizing that they were the only ones he happened to have with him—left over from a little business junket a while back. In this particular case, chutzpah paid off in more than one phony flash in the pan, because before he left he mentioned to some nobody from the class of '56, now the editor of a major New York publishing house, that he'd been "doing a little writing" since he got back. The editor kept after him until he admitted he was almost done with a novel based on his good old college days (which he'd actually written some years before but had been unable to sell). In a blurry haze of Scotch, soda, and old school spirit, the editor promised to publish the book sight unseen. As a writer the guy really was no phony, so he went home, put some new polish on his old nugget, sent it off to his editor friend, and he's been riding in limousines ever since.

# Win Fame as a Bachelor Gourmet Chef

One of Cincinnati's most popular hosts is a middle-aged divorcé I'll call John. John has a local reputation as a gourmet chef, and I once had the distinction of being invited to one of his soirees. It was a bumptuous lot, since the Cincinnati Bengals had just won a football game and everybody was drinking to the team. Someone told me that getting an invitation to one of John's postgame dinners was harder than getting a season ticket to the games themselves. "John's food," the rumor went, "can put you on Cloud Nine."

And yet what was the exquisite dish served that night? Here I was expecting some idiosyncratic bouillabaise, and what the famous chef rolled out was a huge tureen of . . . chili!

One of the simplest dishes in any cookbook. Anybody with a knife and a can opener can make chili, you say.

Not like John's chili. I had to confess it was the best I had ever eaten. With it he served California jug wine, plenty of sourdough bread, and a salad. Just good, simple American food. But not a person there doubted, after tasting John's chili, that He Knew Something They Didn't.

His reputation as a gourmet had been made on that dish, and that dish alone. Sure, he could cook other things, but nothing quite came up to his chili, so at every party he gave he would serve his speciality: that robust, delicious dish that had made his reputation.

John's case is a little extreme, perhaps, but it does illustrate a few basic things about winning fame as a bachelor gourmet chef.

First, a man is not expected to be able to cook at all, so if he can cook so much as one or two really good dishes, he's halfway there—these days he'll win all kinds of praise, especially from appreciative women.

Second, when a man cooks for company it is an exceptional occasion. Keep it that way. If you try to have people over for dinner two or three times a week, not only will the novelty wear off, and some of your reputation with it, but you will have to learn to make twenty or thirty dishes to keep from repeating yourself all the time, which is much too much trouble. Do it every few weeks and you can make it on no more than half a dozen recipes.

Third, any good cook will tell you that cooking is all in the recipes. John claimed he had gotten his chili recipe from a famous restaurateur in Mazatlán, on the promise that he'd never give it away to anyone else. So if you eat something somewhere that you think would be just perfect for making your reputation, get the recipe. Otherwise, you can buy up a bunch of cookbooks and go on a search. If you have a dozen cookbooks in your kitchen, people will never imagine that you can only cook one or two dishes.

Two more things, which are not illustrated in John's example, but which you should keep in mind if you're going to come across as Craig Claiborne instead of Pancho Villa.

Men can get credit for the quality of good ingredients; women can't. If a man goes to an exclusive butcher shop and pays for prime ground meat, that's class. If a woman does the same thing, it's waste—poor home economy. So if you're cooking only once every few weeks, buy the best. As long as you don't mess up the great ingredients, you'll get the credit for that *and* their original quality.

And a man's cooking is greatly enhanced by the appearance of his kitchen. If you put up a pegboard, go down to the local gourmet doodads store, buy up a bagful of wire whisks and cleavers and ladles and garlic presses (a mortar and pestle is great too, but hard to hang up), and adorn your wall with them, your food will taste twice as good as it does now. If you really get carried away, you might even ask the clerk what all this junk you're buying is used for, just so you don't try to beat egg whites with the garlic press. And get yourself an ostentatious spice rack, too.

Furthermore, one little French touch will wow the masses every time and let you put a plain old American dinner across as something straight out of the Tour d'Argent. The favorite of a New York friend of mine is bearnaise sauce. A variation of hollandaise, it is spectacular on London broil which you now call Chateaubriand. So you just get yourself a great, glorious hunk of good red American meat, some Idaho potatoes, a tossed salad and at the last minute you whip up your Béarnaise. *Voila! C'est magnifique!*

Another real *tour de force* is the crêpe or omelet. Get yourself a crêpe griddle or good omelet pan and follow the directions in Fanny Farmer. It's the good old ingredients again; just about anything rich and fancy can go into a crêpe or omelet, so use your imagination. As you cook individual crêpes or omelets, ask your guests (usually brunch) what they'd like in theirs. Making a fantastic crêpe or omelet is fifty times as easy as it looks and impresses people to death.

So if you want to have the reputation of a gourmet chef, you don't have to spend one night a week in cooking school. Just learn how to make one dish—chili, crêpes, or omelets. Add a gallon of wine and a tossed salad and your brunches will be the toast of the town.

95

# Host a Formal Tea

Even though the formal tea is probably the least expensive of all truly elegant occasions, it retains its eminence, among the few who still honor the social graces, as the quintessence of cultured living. The daughters of some of our oldest families still choose to make their entrances into society at one of these traditionally formal functions.

Yet you do not need blue blood to give a tea. All you need are a silver tea service, a linen tablecloth, and a few sandwiches and cookies. The sandwiches should have the crusts removed, be cut into little sections, and should whenever possible be filled with watercress. If you don't have a family silver service and cannot borrow one, you can always rent one and anything else you need by checking the catering services in your Yellow Pages, although if you don't have a linen tablecloth, it is unlikely that any of your friends would be the type to enjoy a formal tea.

To make tea properly you need two pots—one to hold the tea itself, brewed very strong, and one to hold boiling water. In pouring you hold one pot in each hand and blend the tea and water for ''strong'' or ''weak'' or whatever suits each individual guest. If a guest looks at you as though you're crazy, he probably doesn't understand formal teas and when he approaches you with a cup in his hand and regards your two pots with sheepish bewilderment, you should ask, ''Strong or weak?'' He will be grateful at being able to get out of this dilemma just by saying one word or the other, whatever kind of tea he gets. Make sugar, cream (milk for English purists), and lemon slices available to your guests, who can add these extras themselves. But watch for the true tea neophyte, who invariably thinks lemon *and* cream will spice up this pantywaist's concoction.

Although the actual brewing of a perfect pot of tea is not difficult, the rudiments of the procedure are often forgotten, and the result is disaster.

This is especially so among Americans, who were responsible for perfecting that abominable innovation, the tea bag.

Never use tea bags. Always use loose (bulk-pack) tea. Try to employ a little imagination in selecting a brand. There are enough excellent English and Chinese teas on the market that one need never be caught in the embarrassing position of having made a formal setting for Red Rose.

To brew the perfect pot, first scald the teapot with boiling water, empty out the water, and measure in the tea. Now pour more boiling water—it must still be bubbling—over the tea and cover the pot, letting it steep at least four or five minutes before serving. All this, of course, is done in the kitchen a few minutes in advance.

A word, lastly, about timing. If you are planning *a tea* for company on whom the significance of tradition is not lost, you should keep English customs in mind. In the mother country "a tea" consists of tea and biscuits, crumpets, etc., and is served in the late afternoon. "High tea," which many Americans mistake for a more high-class affair, is really a working-class "Sunday night supper," in which two birds, tea and light supper, are killed with one stone. "High" just means "late"—a high tea happens in the early evening, when the man of the house gets home from work. For a really formal tea, don't deviate too far from the "standard" hour of four o'clock sharp. The traditional society tea is not a free-form affair. It does not begin at noon, nor end at nine. Indeed, in England if you start much before three or much after five, you will have no chance of ever being invited to the Palace, because everyone will know you're a bumpkin.

# Form Your Own Society

Have you ever been intimidated, mystified, or otherwise impressed by people who belong to exclusive societies—anything from the Colonial Dames to the local Chillingworth Society for the Arts?

Well, if you have been, that's the idea. Personally I belong to a whole gaggle of these groups, many of which require (on their applications, anyway) that your ancestry be such-and-such, that you have done so-and-so, that this or that person sponsor you, etc. Now, some of them are quite pleasant, actually, and do constructive things now and then. But many do have chilling effects far beyond their actual exclusiveness on those who have been excluded.

If you would like the status of not having to leave blank lines on applications that ask what societies you belong to, or of having something to come back with when the "society" talk starts at cocktail parties, you don't necessarily have to hop over to your leading local socialite like a compulsive toady and beg for admittance to the Chillingworth Society on bended knee. Just do what the founders of that society did.

John O'Hara, the novelist, once decided that all this society snobbery needed to be put in its place. So as a total joke, he and a friend, in patriotic Princeton, founded the Hessian Relief Society complete with a rosette for the buttonhole.

Another currently famous Philadelphia society is also just such a joke. It has an application form a mile long, which asks such things as, "Name four families of royalty from which you are descended," "List four books you have published," "List six decorations you have received from foreign governments," "Name four heads of state who will serve as your references," etc.

Naturally, when people inquire about joining, they take one look at the application form and faint dead away. They could never compete in that kind of company. Of course, no one in the society could either. The "bylaws," which are not referred to in the application, allow that the board of directors may waive the requirements for an especially worthwhile applicant, which is how all the present members made it in. And which is how lots of people who hand you forbidding applications to their societies made it in, too.

This currently prestigious society *and* the Hessian Relief Society, of course, have never done anything in history at all but meet once a year to get roaring drunk. They have been so secretive and exclusive, however, that those who have been awed that John or Jim were members never so much as questioned what something like "Hessian Relief Society" might mean, or what on earth it *might* do.

So take a tip from O'Hara and his Philadelphia followers. Get a few friends together, find an absolutely terrifying name, spend a few dollars on application forms, and go around excluding all those snobs who've been excluding you.

# Drop Names Without Being a Name-Dropper

At a Georgetown dinner party recently, a lawyer who had served in the Truman administration was giving a small audience the benefit of his years of experience in government. His tales dripped with the names of the rich and powerful. "As I told Dean," he would say; or, "Of course the President *agreed* with me." In the course of his monologue a Washingtonian who had heard all this before excused himself for a few moments, then reappeared with a dustpan and broom. "Never mind me," he explained to the curious guests, "I'm just sweeping up the dropped names."

Unfortunately, in this modern, competitive world, name-dropping is not only increasing, but it is consciously promoted. People *will* respond to powerful names, whether those names are clumsily or skillfully dropped. Name-dropping that would have made you a social leper once in Newport or the Main Line may now get you lionized in Georgetown or Manhattan. So you might as well learn the art of successful name-dropping from the real pros—the Washington power-brokers themselves. Capital insiders call it the "art of negative dropping."

This art is based on the Anglo-Saxon juridical principle known as *contra sui,* which stipulates that a self-serving or clearly tendentious statement commands, and should in law command, less credibility than a statement against the speaker's interests. The idea is that nobody would wish to go to a great deal of trouble telling lies against himself. Any evidence, therefore, that leaks through the screen of the Fifth Amendment must be true! And a bland boast thus becomes much less easy to defend than an effusive, but self-deprecating one. Compare the two statements, ''Ham Jordan asked me for a memo on price supports'' and ''Ham really laced into me for that memo I gave him on Soviet trade.'' While you may be reluctant to believe that your dinner partner, for example, actually knows such a luminary as Ham Jordan, you will readily convince yourself it is true if she seems to have mentioned his name at some expense to herself.

The best way to imply that you know Gore Vidal well is to suggest he hates your new hair style. The best way to imply intimacy with Giscard d'Estaing is to say blushingly that he thought your latest economic proposals were *outre et bizarre*.

Watch the TV talk shows. Observe the actress describing how she burnt the casserole when James Beard came to dinner, or how she quite accidentally used a double entendre while chatting with the new Spanish King. What can you come up with to berate yourself? Did you ever get a run in your stocking as you were being presented to Princess Grace? Is your buddy Ralph Nader always accusing you of cheating at poker?

Remember that the secret of successful name-dropping is to let yourself take a fall even as the mention of the celebrity is hoisting you right up with the stars.

# Bluff When You Know the Face but Not the Name

There used to be a Judge in upstate Pennsylvania who was famous for the wide circle of his acquaintances. He had the reputation of never forgetting a face, and yet this reputation was built not on a good memory, but on a technique of greeting guests, hosts, and passersby all with an eager, bonhomie glee.

The Judge as far as I know died without anyone ever finding out that he could barely remember his own name, much less those of the myriad faces who called him friend. A few days before he passed away, he imparted to me the secret of his success.

"Jamie," he said, "there's three ways to say hello. If you've known his name like your own, shake his hand. If you recall the face but haven't a clue to the name, grab his hand between yours and hold on like he's a boyhood chum you haven't seen in twenty years. If you can't recall the face *or* the name, throw an arm around the guy's shoulder and squeeze like the emotion of the moment has left you speechless."

The secret of the Judge's success is simple—what you lack in appellation you make up with affection.

Of course, if you don't like pawing people or hugging hangers-on, you might try one device of a Senator friend of mine. He says, "I have a pamphlet I want to send you. Give me your card."

Whatever you do, don't bluff yourself off a cliff. My grandmother had a friend who recognized an old school acquaintance on a train. During the train-ride conversation, the woman repeatedly mentioned her dear brother.

Just as they were about to disembark my grandmother's friend felt obliged to respond when her train companion alluded to how hard her brother was working.

"And what is your dear brother doing?"

"He still is President of the United States," was the icy response of Theodore Roosevelt's sister.


# Escape When Cornered at a Cocktail Party

I remember being cornered once in Georgetown by a young liberal lawyer who thought the country was going to sink under the Continental Shelf tomorrow if I didn't promise him I would "at least think about" his harebrained schemes for urban renewal. "It's your future too!" he kept yelling until I either had to get out of there or tell him what a boob I thought he was. As I recall, I merely lifted his glass from his hand, announced, "You need a freshener," and slinked away through the crowd toward the punch bowl.

Often, such a simple ruse will work. Not infrequently, however, it will fail, and your unwanted interlocutor will be at your heels all the way to the drinks. Within thirty seconds you'll be listening to his pathetic blather again, having changed nothing but positions.

A much more direct method of redirecting undesired energies is merely to enlist an outsider on your behalf: deflect the young liberal's attention toward a more likely victim and go to the punch bowl alone. Just grab the arm of the nearest passing stranger, look as if you've just stopped an old and close friend, and announce, "Have I got someone for you to meet!"

If your predator's glass is full and the cavalry seems nowhere in sight, however, you should resort to the time-tested ploy: the counterattack. Fight down your bewilderment at his statistics, then suddenly exclaim, "What you're saying just reminded me!" And start on about whatever personal concern of yours would most discomfit him. If your persecutor has been talking about milk price supports, the ideal *non sequitur* might be, "Oh, my cousin Johnny drinks a lot of milk, and I'll tell you, it must be good." If he's been getting rhapsodic, go for something like waste disposal. If he's just reached a plateau of abstraction, bring him down to earth by quoting Blake on "seeing the world in a grain of sand," and begin expostulating on the amazing construction of the starfish.

Get on that hobby horse and ride it for all it's worth. Refuse to let him get in a word edgewise. Make every effort to convince him that the difference between understanding a starfish and understanding the universe is merely a matter of semantics. Eventually he will be struck by the overwhelming desire to tell you what a boob he thinks you are.

And at that point, with any luck, he will grab your glass and rush away to the punchbowl.

# Signal the End of Your Own Party

It is 3:00 A.M. You have just endured hearing an ancient Frank Sinatra ballad for the fourth time in a row. The only peanuts left are being ground into your newly cleaned carpet by a moony-eyed, sleepy couple. The punch bowl is filled with cigarette butts. On the sofa a freshman Congressman is trying to impress a weary secretary from the Nigerian Embassy with his empathy for the Third World. In the corner, slumped within gin-stained clothes, a visiting Dayton businessman is crying, along with Old Blue Eyes, about his lost youth.

Since you have been smiling at these folks since nine o'clock, you are twice as weary as the secretary. As you put on a fifth pot of coffee and sit at the kitchen table, you ask yourself the hostess's oldest, most poignant question:

Why the heck don't they go home?

Hopeless as the situation may appear, the canny hostess's resources are not really limited to silent prayer and occasional glances at her wrist. A little imagination can work wonders. Imagination, tact, and a sense of humor.

England's Queen Elizabeth, for example, has polished to perfection the thankless task of showing her guests the door. But even in her private parties at Windsor and Sandringham she is deft in her approach. At the appropriate hour—which is to say, any hour when the Queen has had enough—she subtly steers the course of the conversation to her guests' lines of work. Inevitably talk turns to the hours of this work, and the items on the next day's agenda.

At this point the Queen gently rises. Her guests, of course, rise as well. And from there it is but a skip and a bow out the door. If any of the guests should suspect that their departure has been Her Majesty's idea, their suspicion is quickly dispelled by the graciousness with which the sovereign ushers them out. Not only are her farewells invariably warm-hearted; they are considerably drawn-out as well, so the guests go away convinced that the idea of leaving was their own, and that the Queen wanted them to remain.

This approach, of course, requires exceptional subtlety, and its success is hardly hampered by Her Majesty's royal position. However, even on the off chance that you are not a Queen, all is not lost. Where the blood royal is lacking, imagination must serve.

I once knew a famous New York host who, when his guests had overstayed their welcome, merely let out from a locked back room his small but extremely friendly schnauzer, Potsy. Potsy was notorious for a single embarrassing handicap: he was unable to distinguish the crossed leg of *homo sapiens,* male or female, from the proffered rump of *canis Schnauzerianus,* female.

The favored guest would shoo Potsy off. Potsy would remain determined. Eventually, his embarrassment triggering some recognition of the late hour, the guest would leave. The host would apologize ("I don't know what gets into him") and hand the victim his coat. Potsy would then move on to a second guest, and so on until the room was cleared.

Less radical measures have been known to achieve equally fast results. The time-honored ruse of placing some appropriate nightcap music on the stereo—say "Good Night Irene" or "The Party's Over"—is still exploited with some effect in the best of homes. Should your tastes, however, incline toward indirection, you might, in the case of winter parties, simply open up all the windows. At other times of the year you might haul out the vacuum cleaner and go after those nuts, or pass out on the floor—this last ruse is sure to elicit both tender ministrations and hasty exits. An eccentric Philadelphia matron known for her large collection of Orientalia was accustomed to rolling into the parlor, at a suitably late hour, a huge Chinese gong. She would strike this with a mallet and announce in clarion tones: "Breakfast is now being served in the street."

Of course, the mask of eccentricity covers a good deal of tactlessness, but there is, after all, no hard and fast rule about these things, since you are dealing with people who have refused to acknowledge the inevitable.

What would I do with the Congressman and his prey and the swooning couple? Offer them back bedrooms, perhaps. Either they would take you up on it and be out of your hair, or cry "Fault" and be out the door. The Drunken Daytonian? Most guests in this condition can safely be handled as if they were incapable of handling themselves. Get an address from his wallet, call him a cab, send him off. He'll probably wake you at ten the next day to apologize.

# Use Handwriting Analysis as a Social Icebreaker

Some years ago I attended a party in Los Angeles where I knew no one and everyone else was acquainted through the film industry. Yet after an hour every starlet in the place was lined up waiting for me to analyze her handwriting, and by the time the evening was done, I'd developed personal relationships with dozens of new people.

Over the years I have found that nothing approaches handwriting analysis as a social icebreaker. I've had many tabs picked up by maître'd's who noticed that I was enlightening waitresses on what their writing revealed about them, and who wanted their own handwriting looked at. Bartenders who've seen me advising the more attractive members of their clienteles (and keeping them around drinking a little longer than they might have) have given me free drinks in exchange for their own readings. Stewardesses have insisted on moving me to empty seats in first class. All I usually have to do is start the usual impersonal conversation about the weather, or really any topic at all, and then say something like, "I'll bet your handwriting is interesting." From there it's a short step to the person's writing a sample. My standard is to have her write, "Now is the time for all good men to come to the aid of the party," "I am happy," and her signature . . . always on unlined paper.

I have never claimed to be a graphologist. When people ask, "Oh, are you a handwriting expert?" I say, "No, but I've fooled around a lot with it"—which is true. You don't have to be an expert to know something about it, and if you study the person carefully as you start in

105

on her writing, you may observe some general traits which will help you interpret or qualify what you find in the writing. Does she come off as an extrovert or an introvert? Does she seem fussy about her appearance or not? Do her clothes or make-up indicate vanity? Do her clothes suggest a high level of education or extensive travel? Does she seem nervous, intense, or fidgety? Does he seem like a precise bookkeeping type who's a stickler for details, or does she come off as someone whose enthusiasm suggests flair and imagination? And so on. Once you have a preliminary feel for the type of person you are dealing with, make your observations about her writing slowly, giving her time to add her own comments as she will. Everything she says may help your descriptions of other traits.

The general rules of thumb I use for the actual analysis are pretty simple. The writing of an extrovert, a person who shows feelings, will slant to the right, and the letters will be fairly large. Vertical or slightly backhand writing suggests a skeptical mind, fairly realistic, not given to going out on or jumping off limbs. Small cramped writing indicates a methodical, perhaps even up-tight personality. A dramatic backhand suggests the subject has overcome shyness. Writing that slopes downward on the blank paper indicates pessimism, and the reverse, optimism. Angular writing (where $a$'s, for instance, come to a point) suggest competitive, ambitious drive, while $a$'s that look like fruit or breasts suggest a more sensuous person, perhaps given to spells of indolence. Unconnected letters imply impulsiveness. $T$'s that are not crossed and undotted $i$'s may mean the person doesn't finish what she starts. Very large capitals suggest insecurity; very small ones, almost the same height as the following letter, hint at self-doubt. Hooks at the beginning of small letters such as $a$'s or $t$'s imply an acquisitive or materialistic nature. Long slashes through $t$'s show stubborness; slashes that cross at the top or above the $t$'s could mean high expectations or even fantasy. Words that end with upward tails suggest feelings that are easily bruised, with the hurts long remembered. Firmly closed letters indicate discretion; too many many letters left open at the top ($a$'s, for example) can point to indiscretion, or a carelessness with the truth. A big capital $I$ means a strong ego—a very small $I$ means a weak one.

Finally, look at the loops above and below the line. Fat above-the-line loops in $f$'s, l's, and $h$'s suggest cerebral imagination. Fat below-the-line loops correspond with below-the-belt—strong libido. Any $y$, $g$, or $f$ that extends deeply below the line can be interpreted as love of adventure, travel, or willingness to experiment. A loop below the line that is closed off short might suggest frigidity or fear of letting feelings go. A strong, straight line extending down deep in an *f, y,* or *g* suggests an active and adventurous person who might sublimate her physical passion in her work.

Then look at the signature. A signature with big capitals and hurried, slurred remainders is apt to be that of an executive who has to write her signature many times a day. A too-fancy signature indicates frustrated creative talent, or an overwhelming love for center stage. A plain one, on the other hand, can show a lack of vanity and a no-nonsense approach to life.

These basics of handwriting analysis will be more than enough to let you use the technique as an icebreaker, and in fact you will seldom use them all. Pick only two or three of the obvious traits in the subject's writing and expand. If she is an extrovert, say, "You like people—you don't like to be alone. You like to go to parties." If she writes small, neatly, and compactly, observe that she is "careful," "methodical," "reliable," a "good employee," etc.

Finally you will need a general conclusion. I try to decide whether the subject is turned on most by heart, mind, or glands. A variation is to say whether a person is generally affectionate, sensuous, or passionate. (Sensuousness will be shown by fat *a*'s, passion by fat loops below the line, and affection by rolling, feminine script.)

If you want more tips, of course, a good book on handwriting will provide them . . . but "just for fun" you'll probably find you don't need them. Just remember—never say anything really bad about a subject. You're not a professional, not a real authority at all. "Tight" should be "careful with money"; "self-hatred," "self-doubt"; "loud" is merely "extroverted"; etc. Don't analyze drunks (their handwriting is bad), foreigners (their writing is different), or printers (impossible).

Try it the next time you need to break some social ice. You'll find people will nod at almost everything you say, if only because there is a hunger in everyone to hear about themselves. Soon an acquaintance you just met will become a friend who'll reveal her whole life story.

# Make Small Talk in an Awkward Situation

Jean Humes, the wife of my cousin John, once told me that the State Department should brief the wives of diplomats on the art of making small talk. When John Humes was our Ambassador to Austria, Jean's protocol duties included calling on the wives of other envoys. "Jamie," she said, "the State Department briefs the wives on all the current foreign problems—none of which we are allowed to talk about. What they ought to do is give you courses on flowers, furniture, and the weather. Those are the only safe things for us to talk about."

She then told me of the time she had paid a formal call on the wife of a newly arrived Ambassador from an Iron Curtain country. The couple lived in a barren apartment with only a cardtable and four chairs for furniture. Her call coincided with a similar visit by the wives of two European envoys. Unfortunately, the French Ambassador's wife talked about the weather, and the wife of the Italian Ambassador asked what flowers their hostess raised in her garden back home. By the time the burden of conversation shifted to Jean, she found herself at a loss for another safe subject. "But then," she told me, "I happened to look up and notice that the ceiling of the barren apartment was very interestingly carved. So I said, 'Madam Ambassador, do workmen in your country still carve such fine work as this ceiling of yours?' "

Jean had known that this "safe question" would bring forth more than a yes-or-no answer, which is the key to making small talk. Communists are sensitive about the level of craftsmanship in socialist societies, and they will dwell at great length on the continuing crafts. So the Ambassador's wife did, and Jean had more than upheld her protocol function.

Jean did have a valid point about offering briefing programs on how to talk about the weather. Climate is always a safe subject in an awkward moment. But the real trick is to ask questions that summon forth more than simple yes-or-no answers. So do not ask, "Was it really $-31°$ outside this morning?" Instead try, "What do you think is causing the old weather patterns to change?" Or, "What are you doing to keep fuel costs down in this cold spell?"

Finding conversational gambits is like defensive tennis. You don't try to kill the ball. Just return it to the other court.

# Squelch an Insufferable Bore

A particularly sharp-tongued friend of mine—a polished veteran of the Prep School Sarcasm Wars—is forever relieved of the burden of frittering away the endless, meaningless, tedious, trivial, and otherwise undesirable hours which many of us more considerate mortals spend writhing in the merciless clutches of relentless bores. At a recent convention we attended together, I got the exact secret of his Houdini-like escapes and merciless put-downs when I saw him in action against a politician who was droning on about the engineering specifications for a dam in Argentina.

"For the past three years," the bore said, going on his sixth or seventh uninterrupted minute, "we've been trying to get the Argentinian government to waive a restriction on the materials to be used for the phlijymongy pfleugergates, but unfortunately the underpass isn't stiff enough to qualify. Now . . ."

"Excuse me," my friend interjected, with a note of some little emergency. "I just noticed my wife is in trouble. Some insufferable bore is chewing her ear off. I really must go rescue her."

My friend, who wasn't even married, was instantly released, with his victimizer's red-faced blessing.

# Deflate an Impossible Snob

There is a much more efficient and fun way to deflate snobs than holding your nose, saying, "Whew! What a stinking snob you are!" and turning on your heel. This method is not so bad when the snobbery is directed at you, because nothing you do is going to change that snob, and chances are if you can't stand his habit to begin with, you don't care what he thinks of you; you just don't want to see him any more.

But if you are present when someone else is being snobbed on, and it bugs you but you are up for a little sporting fun—just agree with everything the snob says, and expand upon it, until you've obviously got him ascending to the heights of the ludicrous. At that point you are ready to make him discover that he's just snobbed on himself. The technique is known in philosophy as the *inflatio ad absurdum,* the "inflation to absurdity," and it's an especially neat cocktail-party trick.

The idea came to me from the same friend who pulls the "bores" trick (which he says can be adapted for snobs too), who related how he'd picked it up at a cocktail party at a yacht club in Rumson, New Jersey. The characters were The Snob, a middle-aged matron who was extremely proud of her lavish garden and of a few articles she'd had published in the local paper (about how to be a garden-snob), and The Wag, who was getting sick of her denunciations of those poor clods who didn't know the difference between a daffodil and a dahlia.

"The absolute *worst,*" she was saying in her most hoity-toity tones, "are those people who mix rutabaga and broccoli in with the perennials. Really, I do think there is nothing quite vulgar as one who plants *vegetables* in one's garden."

She had made the word *vegetables* sound like a newly discovered and particularly virulent intestinal disease. My friend The Wag, jumping at the *inflatio ad absurdum,* agreed with her at once. "Oh, you're quite right," he said. "I couldn't agree with you more. God, what could be

110

worse than stumbling upon a parsnip right next to one of your prize roses? But you *know,*" he went on in a hushed, conspiratorial tone, "I *have* heard of something even worse. *I've* heard that there are *thousands* of those vulgar people living in the Midwest! Rumor has it that they've planted not only garden plots, mind you, but whole *fields* of those awful vegetables! Corn, wheat, string beans, rutabaga, parsnips—I tell you, it's dis*gust*ing! And not only are they growing the stuff, they're *selling* it, and shipping it *East!* Don't you think," he winked, in closing, "something ought to be done about it?"

# Put Down a Pompous Turkey

Now I would be the last person in the world to deny that pomposity has its practical uses. Following the advice of a very wise man I know whose formula for success is, "Look pompous, son, pompous as an ass; nothing succeeds like pomposity," I wear three-piece pinstripe suits just about all the time. They are at any rate the only clothes my somewhat weighty frame looks completely dignified in. A pompous ass outranks a bore or a snob any time, and for those to whom image is all, I am happy to present a pompous facade. However, I prefer that of the turkey to that of the ass, because it is more patriotic.

On at least one occasion, however, I have been mistaken for a *genuine* pompous ass, and that occasion gave me the quintessential insight into how such creatures are put down.

I was hosting a business dinner with a sometime colleague of mine, a self-styled "radical" who'd graduated from The Hill School ten years after I had and within a few years had taken a sharp left turn, politically speaking. Although we got along fine otherwise, I had the feeling that the trappings of my trade, which included a watch-chain draped delicately across the rotundity of my paunch, somehow offended his revolutionary sensibilities.

Now, my watch-chain does not have a watch on it, but a cigar cutter (see "How to Smoke Cigars like Churchill"), and upon dinner's end, I offered my friendly enemy a cigar. He accepted it with the proviso that Cuban cigars were really the best in the world (i.e., better than the excellent cigar I had offered him), and that he would rather smoke a cigar like Castro than like Churchill (i.e., keep it in his mouth and chew on it instead of puffing away delicately now and again).

So, drawing myself up to my full pomposity, I offered him the service of my cigar cutter. He accepted and handed his cigar over for treatment. With much ceremony and flourish and declamation over the virtues of proper cigar cutters, I brandished my invincible instrument of Anglo-American culture, made the requisite incision, and presented the object of his smoking pleasure back to him.

In total good nature (ostensibly) he laughed heartily, looked from the cigar to me and back again, and said, "Jesus! That cutter gashed the hell out of this poor thing! I could have done better with my teeth!"

Now since he was laughing so generously, I couldn't apply the cutter to his nose, so I had to admit he'd shot the turkey (for one round, anyway) as I found myself lamely regarding the cutter and muttering, "Hmmm. Guess the blade must be dull."

# Be the Intellectual at the Cocktail Party

In the 1950s there was a character who used to strike an intimidating pose at Washington cocktail parties. His weapon was the thin airmail edition of the *Manchester Guardian,* which used to peep out of the pocket of his Harris tweed jacket. This self-anointed intellectual with his briar pipe and British regimental striped tie didn't even have to say anything intelligent. He just mumbled through puffs of smoke the names of certain British members of the intelligentsia like Cyril Connolly, John Osborne, or Kingsley Amis ("Of course Cyril Connolly thinks that's really a very sophomoric approach, doesn't he? Didn't you find delicious his column in the *Spectator?*")

At that time in American literary salons, would-be insiders slavishly took their cues from their British counterparts. Anyone who dressed like Oxford and mouthed the right names was asked his opinion on everything. The only contribution of this pseudo-English character was to either sadly shake his head or nod with the hint of an amused smile, but that was all this poseur (whose only English experience was shaving with Wilkinson blades) had to do.

Today in the 1970s the game is still the same even though the uniforms, the symbols, and the names of the high priests have changed. Now a professor might wear jeans and Gucci loafers or sandals (but in either case sockless), the top might be a designer shirt or turtleneck with a pendant. His bible would not be an English journal but the *New York Review of Books.*

Like the Bible, the *Review* is held in sacred awe even if it's rarely read. All the aspiring egghead has to do before a party is actually read one article in this publication and scan the titles of the other pieces. If you just mention what Dwight Macdonald or George Steiner said in the latest edition, authors will think you a Columbia Ph.D. and Ph.D.'s will suspect that you are a closet poet. If at the last minute before an arty party you can't locate a *New York Review of Books,* then at least pick up yesterday's or today's New York *Times* and read the book review (it is always located on the crossword puzzle page). Don't mention the review to those you meet, just act as if you actually read the book. If you do, the word will be out that you are a real intellectual.

# Make an Effective Complaint

You know the way the TV cops interrogate a potential stool pigeon. They work in teams. The first cop is Mr. Nice Guy. He sits on the desk across from the suspect, runs a hand through wavy hair, offers a cigarette, and begins, "Now, Jim, I hear you've had some trouble. . . ." Then his partner sidles in. His hair is even greasier than the suspect's, and his expression suggests that his shoes are too tight. He's the one who stands behind the suspect's chair, flicks on the gooseneck lamp, and hints that if the punk doesn't come across fast he'll never see daylight again.

The strategy, a variation of the old carrot-and-stick approach, is effective because the buttering-up process puts the victim so much off his guard that when the tough cop threatens him, he turns to the nice one as if he's an ally rather than just another bull, and "spills his guts."

A similar strategy can be used to make a truly telling complaint. The difference is that when you make a complaint you play both cops at once. Either one alone won't do. If you're abusive and threatening to a hopelessly tardy waitress, for example, she may get the bouncer to toss you out. On the other hand, if you're solicitous—if you commit the unforgivable sin of apologizing for complaining—she will know you are uncertain of yourself and merely ignore you.

So make your complaint with a kind of determined pique—but preface it with such elaborate praise of the establishment's previous efforts on your behalf that the entire staff, from the offending party up to the manager, is mortified to have failed in its duty to a steady and honored customer.

If you have been waiting to pay for that bottle of Brut for the past fifteen minutes, don't raise the roof *or* fidget in the corner. Corner the waitress or maître d' and say, "For the twelve years I've had a charge card here, I have always been impressed with the prompt and courteous service. That is why I cannot understand . . ." If the carrots on your plate look more like turnips, it will be, "I've been coming here ever since Pierre opened, and this is the first time the vegetables have ever been overcooked." If the automobile agency has had you on "hold" all through lunch, remind them, when they finally return, that you bought your last three cars from them, but that they're about to lose a customer unless . . .

Eliciting an apology and a promise of "better in the future" is a matter of balancing your righteous ire with that modest ingratiation that any regular customer can summon at will. So say you are a regular even if you are not. And remember that a *faux pas* at your expense is an affront not only to you, the customer, but to the fine establishment whose services you have enjoyed these many years.

# Put People at Ease

One night in a restaurant in Cleveland a business associate and I were discussing how to put people at ease in awkward situations. He claimed his mother had a skill at this high art which was so effortless that it was impossible that anyone could excel her. I challenged him to give an example proving this quite substantial claim, and he did.

My associate had just graduated from Stanford and announced his engagement to a perfectly charming girl he had met there (currently known as his wife). His father, a successful stockbroker, and his mother, an active, urbane socialite, dearly loved their daughter-in-law-to-be. There was only one immediate problem: her father, a widower, was a retired West Virginia coal miner.

Now, this didn't bother my associate's mother. Besides heartily approving of her son's chosen mate, she well remembered that her own grandfather had been a coal miner in Pennsylvania, and she certainly was no snob. But she did spend some time wondering whether there would be any way on earth for the old coal miner to feel comfortable when he drove up their long tree-lined drive and parked his decrepit pickup truck behind her new Continental, and got a load of their nine-room ranch house with the swimming pool in the backyard.

What did she do? Go out and get a jug of moonshine and meet him in the driveway, half crocked, with the Spirit of West Virginia staining her most stylishly tattered jeans?

Get on the power lawnmower and putter over to him with shreds of grass in her hair?

Call her yardman to come over for a drink so her guest would have someone of "his own class" to talk with?

Not a bit of it. She knew that the minute she stopped acting naturally, she'd start wearing her unease on her face and guarantee that she'd make her guest squirm in the throes of mutual embarrassment. After all,

115

creating all kinds of fluster around his arrival would just confirm his fears that he'd stick out like a sore thumb on a concert violinist.

So in preparation she did nothing... except to send her husband across town for a case of beer, and after he left, to let the air out of their Continental's right rear tire.

So the old Dad instead of feeling inadequate to the situation, felt superior, when he saw the new car out of commission. He fixed the tire and they all celebrated his heroics with several brews.

# Break or Refuse a Date

You really *didn't* want to go to the jai alai match with your boss's son, but some quirk of duty to the laws of etiquette and practicality made you say yes anyway. Now Wonderful Person has called, and since you've been waiting for that call, it seems, for most of your life, you'll just have to find some way to break that other date. Without hurting the boss's son's feelings, of course. "Oh, why did I say yes in the first place!" you think, trying to decide whether you should tell the truth to the poor boob or lie. You know, of course, that you'll lie.

Actually, I prefer the lie, at least the off-white lie, to the unvarnished truth in such situations. I would rather have someone say, "Jamie, I just can't go. There's someone very sick in the family," than have to hear, "Jamie, you're a loudmouth bullshitter, and I'm not going out with you." I don't believe there's anything wrong in trying to save a person's feelings, and often when I've been lied to I've actually appreciated it.

If you are going to lie, however—at least about why you are really turning down or breaking a date—get in one good reason and call it quits. If your excuse is weak, stand on it anyway. Never try to make up in quantity for what you lack in quality. You know the kind of line: "Jamie, I'd love to but I think I have a cold coming on. Anyway, my sister may be coming over tonight and I've got those end of the month reports to get out... you know."

Any one of those excuses would be sufficient. But all three? Never. You're a dead giveaway. Even if all of them were true—anyone throwing all that ammunition at once has got to be hiding something.

Whether you think a cold is coming on or not, you say, "I've got a cold coming on. I'm really sorry but the last time this happened and I went out anyway I was in bed for three weeks. Besides, I wouldn't want to give you a cold." Or for a shorter version try, "I'm deathly ill. I think God is punishing me for my sins." Laugh off solicitation with a flippant "the prognosis is that I'll live," uttered with such hoarse degeneration in your voice that your listener is led to suspect that you may already be dead. (If you really want to turn off a romantic pursuer, say you have diarrhea.)

Don't say, "My sister may be coming over," as if she might just stop by for some coffee. No—she called and said she has something important to discuss with you about the family. She sounded almost hysterical, and she's a very level-headed woman. And then call your sister. She hasn't heard from you in ages.

If there's office work to do, do it. But don't make it sound like a couple of contracts the boss asked you to look over. It's the whole end-of-the-month reports, for Heaven's sake, don't make it sound like nothing. Paint a picture of yourself cornered in a room with mounds of paper. Your eyes are blurry, and all you can see is numbers, bills of lading, stock certificates, and more numbers. You're very upset about the whole thing.

The single excuse will work every time—if you make it obvious that there's nothing *you* can do about your reason for refusing or cancelling, whatever it is.

# Get Simple, Satisfying Revenge

My brother once had a top sergeant whose idea of fun was to give his new recruits piles of useless work to be performed each day before sundown, then order them to destroy the products of their labor and begin again. For months my brother was condemned to typing out reams of administrative gibberish under the watchful eye of this sadistic non-com; and each day shortly before mess call, the sergeant would shuffle through the day's work carelessly, hurl the papers on the harassed private's desk, and grump, "Well, kid, it looks like you got another load to do for tomorrow. Rip 'em up."

Now, whereas my brother never quite figured out what this bastard sergeant thought he had to gain from roasting his recruits so regularly, he did come up with a simple and effective way of telling the sergeant what he thought of him. The day after his basic training was over and he was freed from his tormentor's jurisdiction, he merely mailed him, without a return address and without a card, a small box of screws.

A box of screws brightly packaged with wrapping paper and ribbon may be the perfect present for you to give to that bastard or bitch who has tried to do a number on you.

If the rat's conduct calls for more drastic measures, send him a subscription of sado-masochism porn—at the office. Or if it's not worth spending a nickel, call him long-distance collect under another name and emit a loud Bronx cheer and then—hang up.

# Accept Compliments with Grace

A Scottish countess once told me that the best test of a person's "breed-ing" is the way he or she receives a compliment. I was spending the Christmas holidays in a castle near Edinburgh, and one night before a black-tie dinner my hostess, the Countess Balfour, complimented me on my dinner jacket. I looked away, stammering, "It was my father's; it's out of style now."

"James," she said regally, "act like a gentleman when you receive a compliment. Say 'Thank you, I quite like it myself.' " You don't have to say it is your father's jacket, but if you do, say it with pride! "It's my father's from his college days. Amazing how well they made clothes then."

People only reveal their social insecurity by deflecting compliments, and actually the "Oh, it's not so great" response comes across as fishing for further and higher compliments. The person who compliments you doesn't want an argument! Deflecting compliments is a common enough social error, based on the mistaken belief that such behavior implies modesty. But it is actually a slap in the face to the person complimenting you as though you didn't appreciate a kind word. If you must be modest, turn the conversation to the subject of the compliment. Your jacket, your debating championship, your rose garden, and tell some funny anecdote about it at your own expense.

# Respond to a Dear John Letter

To a celebrity like Tallulah Bankhead, a bad review is like a Dear John letter. So the next time you get a missive that dismisses you with prejudice, respond as she did to one bad review. "I am sitting in the smallest room in the house. Your review is before me. Soon it will be behind me."

# Give a Present That Will Always Be Remembered

Any Head of State or Foreign Secretary visiting the United States can count on receiving one or the other of two standard official gifts: a piece of Steuben glass or a piece of Boehm porcelain. While I am personally very fond of Steuben glass, I have repeatedly suggested that the State Department adopt gifts of some greater originality and variety—at least for the visitor's *second* visit. There is no point, it seems to me, in presenting the Israeli Premier with the same token of national esteem that you have presented two weeks before to the Emir of Dubai: all that suggests is that you have a huge carton of secondhand Boehm in a back room that you are rapidly trying to get rid of.

If you want a present to be remembered long after it has been presented, you must strive to come up with something that is personal as well as original, elegant, expensive, etc. This applies to wedding, birthday, and graduation presents as well as to State Department amulets. A little thought can trigger the most peculiar recollections. If you put your mind to it, you will remember that Cousin Harold was always interested in early English history. Why not forget about the pipe and the cardigan and the year's subscription to *Country Living,* and give him instead something he, and he alone, would appreciate: a bound copy of, say, the Star Chamber rolls for 1597?

I am a great believer in the usefulness as gifts of first editions, ancient manuscripts, and original autographs. I don't know how many of my last-minute panics about gift-buying have been cleared by the recollection that the potential recipient was descended from Romanov royalty, or had spent a year studying Welsh in Aberistwyth, or had had a lifelong interest in the Ming Dynasty. To a Governor's daughter who had spent a junior year in Scotland, I once presented an autographed letter by Sir

Walter Scott. To a new Ambassador to Austria I gave a copy of a famous Austrian treaty which I picked up at an autograph house for half the price I might have spent for silver or Boehm. To a U.S. Senator, I gave a chunk of masonry that I had retrieved from the rubble of the original Capitol building, rebuilt in 1959.

The point is that a little imagination will do a hell of a lot more to make your gift memorable than digging deep into your wallet for the standard, expensive gifts. One of the presents I have most enjoyed giving was an autograph that I gave to young Winston Churchill, the grandson of the late Prime Minister, a few years ago. I had heard that young Winston's wife, Minnie, was a direct descendant of the Southern statesman John Slidell. Mary Benjamin, the New York autograph house, located for me a letter written by Slidell when he was Senator from Louisiana. I think it cost me less than $25, and the house kindly threw in an old print of Slidell for no extra charge.

Yet this inexpensive gift, which cost me only a little extra effort—a phone call here, a visit there—turned out, I later discovered, to be among the most prized possessions of the Churchill descendants. Years after I had chosen it, I was in a receiving line next to Minnie after the marriage of young Winston's mother to Governor Averell Harriman of New York. "You know, Pam," Minnie told her mother-in-law, "all of our visitors are anxious to see our Churchill memorabilia. But Jamie's gift is one of the few things in the house that's really mine."

# Write a Real Thank-You Note

When I was first running for the Pennsylvania legislature, Bill Scranton, later Governor and Ambassador to the United Nations, told me, "Jamie, remember—keep you-you-you-ing them in your little campaign talks."

That's good advice for thank-you notes, too. Don't say, "I had such a wonderful time." Instead, make it, "What a fantastic hostess you are!

You do things with such effortless ease." "What fascinating friends you have." "What wonders you have done with the house."

Then pick out one good detail to back up your praise. If you liked her cooking, rave about the soufflé. If you liked the guests, mention one who particularly struck your fancy. Or if it's the house, write about the new draperies or heirloom china.

There is only one thing that makes writing a thank-you note hard, and that is waiting too long to write it. Then you think you have to compose a work of art to compensate for your tardiness. The antidote is—write it now, and keep it short. Start out with "You . . . ." and end up with one or two examples of the hostess's warmth or hospitality.

# Send Flowers with Flair

An acquaintance of my mother's once gave an informal party for Winston Churchill. The buffet was cold fried chicken, an American invention which the aging statesman, whose mother was American, found greatly to his liking. He came to her for seconds.

"May I have a breast?" he asked.

"Mr. Churchill," my mother's friend replied with great restraint, "in this country it is the custom to ask for white meat or dark meat."

"I *am* sorry," Churchill replied.

The following day the hostess received a corsage. On top of the orchid a small card bore the handwriting of the great man himself:

"I would be most obliged if you would pin this on your white meat."

Few in Sir Winston's position would have come up with anything more scintillating than "Thanks for the party. Your servant." The great man, however, had flair: that indescribable something that makes the difference between a risqué charmer and a run-of-the-mill lout. Anyone can send flowers, but it takes a touch of the unconventional to ensure that they will be received as a personal and memorable gift.

Any flower shop will be glad to send a "very special bouquet" for you, but unless you take the trouble to go to the shop yourself and select the particular flowers you want, you may find the next day that the person you had intended to flatter is miffed or brooding over the fact that the token of your esteem includes two faded roses, an enormous clump of statice, and a bunch of scraggly carnations. Unless you specify, even the most reputable shop in the world will send off the things they have not been able to get rid of. And you are hardly going to impress your beloved with a box of last week's leftovers.

But the most important trick in sending flowers with flair is to send them when they're not expected. Forget the flowers on your anniversary—take her out skydiving instead, and send flowers on the anniversary of your first meeting, or when she's just gotten a big promotion. A friend of mine sends his mother a bouquet of chrysanthemums every year on *his* birthday. An unexpected gift of flowers commemorating some special occasion is worth twenty times as much as the usual shipment at the usual time, which usually conveys that you've just taken the easy way out and don't really care.

And finally—always be personal. She's worth it. He's worth it. You're worth it. Take a few minutes to write something poignant, hilarious, or whatever on the card. If your friend is fond of yellow, try yellow roses rather than red. If your first date was on Christmas Eve, a poinsettia will bring it all back. If he's handy in the kitchen, why not send him a planter of chives? Many large plant emporiums have large collections of live spices. Plants in general—herbal or merely decorative—can be every bit as touching as cut flowers, and they will still be around when you're gone. Remember that the smallest bouquet, personally chosen for a special occasion, will be far longer and more deeply appreciated than the largest funereal bloom sent direct from Flo's Flower Heaven.

# Pick Up a Last-Minute Date

It's Saturday afternoon, it's London, and it's spring. Chance has delivered into your hands two tickets to a Covent Garden *Madame Butterfly,* but the performance is that very evening and you know nobody in town. Where do you find the right date before eight?

I once solved this very problem by going to the Royal Academy on Picadilly, hanging around a Cezanne until a likely prospect appeared, and engaging her in conversation about the master's use of light and shade. Then, as if on the spur of the moment, I said, "Look, I'm a stranger in town and I've got these two tickets to the Opera tonight. Do you like Puccini?"

She did, and was delighted to go.

Now I might as easily have done my looking at a zoo, at a lecture, or in the park. Any public place, that is, where the atmosphere is relaxed and where, even if you are only there to spy out a date, there is a common focus of interest, talking is easy, and you can make it seem as though picking up a date is the last thing on your mind. And she can, too.

The main lesson here is to stay away from bars. The infamous "singles bars" of New York City's East Side are proof enough of the new adage "Seek too hard and ye shall not find." Where everybody is admittedly looking for somebody else—men for one-night stands, women for the perfect marriage partner, or vice versa—the bar turns into a bargain basement. Everyone is more paranoid about being mistaken for cheap goods than open to real relations. And if it should come out in a bar that you're looking for a date to the opera, you'll probably get laughed out of the house anyway.

So unless you want to endure Puccini alone, use your head. Stay out of the meat markets. Go to a neutral spot and keep your eye out for that stray, preoccupied lamb. Look preoccupied yourself, and the date will take you both by surprise.

# Dine in Style as a Woman Alone

There really is nothing wrong with a woman dining out alone, although people certainly seem to think there is, because you so seldom see it done. Or perhaps the problem is that women are afraid it's always going to *look* wrong, as though the lone woman diner is running away from home or has been unable to get a man to take her out, and at the last minute has failed even to collar a girlfriend she can drag along for company and/or "protection."

Whatever the reason, however, it certainly is a shame that so many women travelling in strange cities hole up in their hotel rooms, order dinner from room service, and turn in early, instead of venturing out in style to restaurants they've heard about and really would like to try. And consider the woman whose husband and/or family is out of town, or who just wants to be alone with her food and her thoughts for one evening. If you think about it, it's obvious that what makes the difference between your being mistaken for a lonely, desperate piece of wolf-bait or being seen as an independent, distantly intriguing, even vaguely regal figure, to be approached with courtesy and discretion if at all—is the way you go about it.

First, your attitude, and what it implies. Consider the advantages of dining alone and be prepared to enjoy them. You can concentrate on the meal itself, and you can observe your surroundings and the other diners in peace, without the constant need to make talk (small or large) between each bite. You can think your own thoughts for a change. You can take a mini-vacation.

This implies, however, that you go to a place where the food is actually worth your close attention. You are never going to make it savoring every delicious bite of the special of the day at Buggsy's Beanery. So pick a first-rate French restaurant, or a gourmet northern Italian establishment (where cannelloni and saltimbocca alla romana outsells spaghetti and meatballs), or an elegant Continental dining place. And try to find a restaurant with a good wine list and a real wine steward. If you are looking to luxuriate, full service and good wine is as essential as the food and surroundings.

When you call to make your reservation—if you have a title, by all means use it. It is not a bad idea to use Professor or Doctor even if you aren't one, because these people's professions often explain why they are in strange cities (for conventions or whatever) and why they might prefer to dine alone now and then. Not to mention the "status" advantages, or the fact that the hors d'oeuvres will probably come more quickly if the waiter thinks you're a mean hand with a scalpel. Otherwise, use "Ms." Nowadays most professional women do, married or not. Or you can use just your name—"Caroline Brady"—as an actress or other artist might do.

If you have any doubts about the restaurant's wine selection, ask to speak to the wine steward on the phone, and make sure he has something you'll want to drink in your price range. When you get there he will remember you, greet you as though he knew you, and you will have a head start on the game.

As to dress, it can be anything from a tailored suit with a little more flair and style than the average—set off by some extra touch like a hat, neck scarf, or jewelry (which dispels the idea that you've run straight over from the funeral directors' convention)—to the kinds of things an avant-garde actress might wear. Suit yourself, as long as you create an aura that shows you *have* suited yourself. You may look alluring, but above all you do not want to look like a lure. "Self-contained elegance" is really what you're after. You have dressed explicitly to dine out alone.

When you arrive at the restaurant, find out (perhaps when you check your coat) the name of the maître d'. He and the sommelier and the waiter will probably be the closest things you have to dinner companions, so you should give them every chance to be personable and pamper you with their finest "old world" treatment. Call them by their first names. (Which is "the way it is done" in the best restaurants anyhow.) If you are curious about the restaurant, the chef, the neighborhood, etc.—ask them. Discuss your meal and wine with them. What do they recommend for a leisurely full-course dinner? Ask to be seated at a banquette, which places you in earshot intimacy with other diners.

Look happy, even if you're not. Don't read a book, as though you're fighting boredom or loneliness. Instead, you might take a small notebook and write. Write anything; laundry lists, poetry, notes on what you are going to do for the next week, snatches of your latest autobiographical novel. You are thinking, observing, and enjoying. Others in the restaurant will wonder not whether you decided on dinner here instead of a suicide attempt, but whether you are a journalist, a fashion designer, or an unrecognized visiting celebrity.

If you want to encourage conversation with those at tables around you, try asking the waiter (so the others can overhear) whether there's a good art gallery open nearby, or what is the quality of the local symphony orchestra or ballet group. Just make it easy for others to help you out (and satisfy a little of their curiosity about you) by volunteering some information about their city. People love to talk about the cultural assets of their own city to strangers, especially Easterners. It never hurts to order a full bottle of wine instead of a half (which looks a little skimpy). You don't have to drink it all, and you will find asking an interested couple—be it husband and wife or two gentlemen—to share it with you much more delicate than offering to buy them a round of stingers.

Depending on how exotic you want to appear, you might keep in mind that a cape and/or a large, wide-brimmed hat immediately evoke images of mystery and romance, but at the same time suggest that you do value your privacy.

Dining alone in style is actually a sort of secret ball for women who know how to carry it off. So whether you'd prefer to sweep in surrounded by that air of exotic mystery, cause the whispers of romantic speculation to buzz all around you, enjoy your dinner, and sweep away again into the night; or whether you'd rather meet the people around you, offer them some wine, and maybe have them invite you for a cruise on their yacht the next day—you need never again fear being ''seen alone'' in a restaurant.

# "High-Noon" Your Lunch Hour

A bored secretary once quit her job at the Department of Agriculture and took a job as a Kelly girl. She arranged her stints so she could work as a lunchtime hat-check girl in a restaurant next door to the Senate Office Building. Before long she could recognize many of the Senators who ate there. "Senator Tower," she would say, "that was quite a story about you and the astronauts." Or, "Senator Hollings, you look even more distinguished than your pictures."

After about a year and a half of this blarney, she was on speaking terms with twenty-five Senators and a host of other notables. Then she applied for a TV job in Philadelphia. With the help of letters of recommendation from several of her congressional acquaintances, she soon landed an assistant producer's slot on a daytime interview show. The management evidently figured she had the necessary connections to wangle TV appearances by the famous—and so she did.

This is what I call "high-nooning" your lunch hour. And anybody can do it.

Those sixty minutes out of the office each day are precious. Why waste them? Why spend half of them eating a tuna-fish sandwich in the local drugstore, and the other half browsing through the fan magazines? Why not pack a lunch and set out for an adventure?

A Philadelphia woman I know used to spend her hour at the stock exchange. Each day she would come with her lunch and follow the ticker. The young brokers were only too eager to explain the big board's shorthand symbols to her, and eventually she saved enough by not buying lunch that she was able to purchase her own $15 stock certificate.

High-nooning can include almost anything. A would-be artist friend of mine goes to the Philadelphia Art Museum (which lets her keep an easel and brushes there) and copies paintings. Many passerbys, she reports, seem more interested in her work than in the originals. Another friend takes a paper bag to the local symphony hall on days when the orchestra rehearses; he now counts as friends two violinists, three flutists, and a French horn.

The possibilities of adventure are endless. Go to that book-autographing session being advertised by the local department store. Or look in your TV listings to see what author is appearing today on the noon talk show. Buy her book and bring it to the studio for an autograph. You will find you're the only audience there, and she will probably be so pleased at your interest she'll ask you out for a drink.

Whatever you do, don't squander that precious hour at a lunch counter. Go where the action is.

# Wangle Nights Out Alone

Some years ago a businessman who lived in a Washington suburb was feeling cramped by his routine, split-level existence. He loved his wife but he yearned to have just one night a week out alone. One Saturday morning as he was picking up a tux for a party, the sight of an adjacent Army-Navy store gave him a brilliant inspiration. He had served three years in the Navy. The following week he went to the store and purchased a secondhand lieutenant's uniform. Then he came home and told his wife that he had enrolled in the Naval Reserve. The additional benefits in insurance and pensions, he explained, would provide them with a nest egg for their old age. Unfortunately, he would have to spend every Thursday evening away from home.

For the next several months, every Thursday after dinner the businessman would kiss his wife, change into his uniform, and trot off on a survey of some of the town's more interesting nightspots. The wrench only was thrown into this innovative admiral's plans six months later, when his wife one day informed him, "I ran into another Naval Reservist. He says you'll have to go on a two-week cruise this summer! What's *that* going to do to our *vacation plans?*"

I hear that they took separate vacations, and that the wife is now considering taking karate on Fridays. Be that as it may, the moral is clear: if you need a night out alone, the secret is routine. Whether it's bowling every Tuesday or yoga every Saturday, keep the schedule consistent. Go out only on "your" night, and stay out for the same hours each time.

My recommendation, furthermore, is to be honest, and really enroll in that business administration course or that French cooking class. Of course, unless one finds a preponderance of the opposite sex disconcerting to one's study habits, the man might want to learn about cuisine and the woman about corporations.

# Meet Rich Playboys

About a year ago a young lady who had read "How to Put Adventure in Your Life," an article I'd written for *Glamour* magazine, came to my office. She didn't want legal advice. She wanted to know how she could meet wealthy men. I told her I wasn't *that* kind of counsellor, but I agreed to give her ten minutes' worth of free advice.

She lived at home and worked for the state, so she had had few opportunities to meet the type of man she was looking for. She had, however, saved up some money for a vacation, and so I decided to tip her off to the names of the current "in" spots for damsels in such distress. Gstad, I said, had faded, and Hong Kong was just too far. If she was really determined to get scooped up by a sugar daddy, she should book a flight for Acapulco, Aspen, or Marbella.

"Bonnie," I told her, "forget the young men. Even if they're rich—which is unlikely—the competition will be too fierce for you to hack in a two-week vacation. Keep your eye out for somebody about twenty years older than you. Shrug off the young ones' advances—remember, you're not going there for a good time. Look as if you're alone—which you will be—and discreetly available. Adopt a demure, even serious manner. The best way to do that is to take along a good book—something that will invite comment and discussion. Not Tolstoy or Jane Austen, but something substantial from the older men's own era. Hemingway or John O'Hara would be ideal. Spend at least two or three hours a day engrossed in the book. Whether you do this on the beach, by the pool, or at the bar is immaterial. The thing to remember is that you want to appear preoccupied, as if all those Croesuses milling around you are of no greater interest than the waiters. Then, when one of them does come up to you to talk—and they will—you will not appear a golddigger at all, but a shy librarian off on a busman's fling.

"Eventually, Bonnie, you'll find a nice-looking older man reading over your shoulder. And from there," I winked slyly, "you're on your own!"

Well, Bonnie did not take a book by Hemingway. Instead she picked a book about Hitler. And she did not go to Acapulco but to the Cape. She did not attract somebody fantastically rich, but he was respectable and eligible.

Her new middle-aged friend had fought in World War II in Europe and was happy to have the chance to share some of his war exploits with her. After the vacation they continued their relationship by writing and by frequent visits.

They haven't married—yet.

# Pub-Crawl in a Strange City

First, you must find a real pub. Not just any bar will do. The pub may be a neighborhood bistro, the drinking salon of a French restaurant, or the local factory workers' hangout. But it must have what has so often, and with inevitable imprecision, been referred to as "atmosphere." *Ambience,* the French say. This can consist of bullfight posters on the walls, or a brass rail from an old firehouse, or simply a garrulous, witty bartender. It should not include such peculiarly American gaucheries as neon lights, Formica tabletops, or chrome.

Ask a native which bar has the most atmosphere. Follow your informant's directions and find the pub where you will begin your crawl. After a few drinks, ask the owner to direct you to Square Two. Where does he go to relax? You'll be leaving tomorrow morning, want to do a bit of wandering. Is there a place within walking distance?

Go to the second place. Repeat procedure until you lose count of pubs and/or until your eyes try to convince you that you have wandered back into Pub Number One. At this point, it would probably be a good idea to ask for directions to your hotel, although any inveterate pub-crawler, London-style, will refuse to clear out until the traditional ten minutes after the bartender has given the third last call.

Each foreign port has its own delights, and it would be presumptuous to detail the attractions of the "ideal" pub crawl. Different people, of course, do it for different reasons. Most, however, would admit that their attachment to the peripatetic night out is based on a desire to (1) take in as many unfamiliar sights as possible while (2) remaining just alert enough to be able to see them.

Within those broad parameters, the attractions of the rummy road are many. You will discover that in Amsterdam chilled gin (not bathtub gin, but real Ginebre) costs about as much as beer. In the north of England and in Scotland and Ireland, many small towns have their own breweries, and you can sample, in the course of a night's crawling, not only the conglomerate's brands but a whole range of local potions, which are invariably tastier and more potent. In Barcelona you can purchase ten ounces of Spanish brandy at a *bodega* for about fifty cents, then proceed to the next *bodega* much fortified, and so on into the dawn.

Perhaps the most famous pub-crawling area in the world is Rose Street in Edinburgh. Almost fifty bars line the twelve blocks between Princess and George streets. The wise crawler avoids those that look like American imitation, entering only those in which the Tudor beams are made of wood rather than Contac. Throughout Scotland and England, American blended whiskey is difficult to come by. If you wish Scotch, order "whisky." If you want what Americans call whiskey, better confer with the bartender; it's very likely he can recommend a good local concoction that will be to your taste.

Pub-crawling is no longer an exclusively European diversion. Probably as a result of the increase in transatlantic travel in recent years, the sport has made an appearance in cities and towns from Duluth to Tallahassee. A widely travelled friend of mine insists that New York is the pub-crawler's paradise. "Between the United Nations on the East Side and Port Authority on the West," he says, "there's more Irish pubs than in all of Dublin."

# Make a European Hotel Your Executive Mansion

The great thing about going to good European hotels such as the Connaught in London, the Bristol in Paris, the Gritti in Venice, or D'Angleterre in Copenhagen, is that you can be made to feel like you're a visiting prince or business tycoon. Actually, if you know the secret, the whole hotel complex and personnel can become in effect your personal staff.

The secret is the head porter or concierge. He is much more than a veteran master sergeant. He is a magician. At a wave of his hand, theater tickets are found, a limousine is reserved, flowers are sent, gifts are delivered. But you can't just wave a five-dollar bill and turn this dynamo on. He is a proud man, used to assisting sultans and statesmen. Because he is a professional, he will do a serviceable job for any hotel client. But what you want to do is make him an ally and associate.

The best way of accomplishing that is what a lawyer friend of mine did at the Excelsior in Rome a few years ago. He engaged the concierge in conversation the first evening and said that he wished to hire a limousine and driver the next morning to go to Castel Gandolfo. (Castel Gandolfo is the summer residence of the Pope.) The next morning, the concierge had the car awaiting at his disposal. "Good morning, *Consigliore*, I hope your meeting with His Holiness goes satisfactorily." Actually, my friend did not go to see the Pope at all. He spent the afternoon touring the countryside around Rome along the ancient Roman road, the Via Appia Antica. But his rental was well spent because he had impressed the concierge that he was a man of eminence who deserved and would appreciate all the amenities of service. (The chauffeur, who doesn't deal with the concierge directly, wouldn't breach ethics and say anything.)

To establish yourself you could, at Claridge's in London, ask the attending porter to order a car to go to Checquers (the Prime Minister's country residence); or at the Palace in Brussels, say to the concierge that you have an appointment at NATO headquarters, which is a thirty-five kilometer ride.

Of course you don't have to go to such lengths. Just enlist the concierge in a conversation on the first day of your visit. Ask him where you can have shoes made or where you might find some antique French Haviland to complement your own china collection. But whether it's engaging a local university history professor for an afternoon tour or arranging a transatlantic call to Washington, be sure to show the concierge or head porter you are a discriminating traveler of wide experience. He will work hard to show you he is the equal or better of anyone else in his profession.

# Get Cabs on Rainy Days

If it looks as if God has broken the covenant with Abraham and you've been huddling under a dripping awning for the past half hour, there are two things you should remember. One: empty cabs go downtown on the biggest and/or fastest city arteries possible. And two: cabs converge on major hotels, along with bus and train stations. But at stations and other "public" cab stands, you can get no special advantages, and in fact you are at a disadvantage without luggage, which would suggest to the cabbie that you may be a customer for a long and lucrative ride.

So if you're stuck for a cab on a rainy day, first figure out whether you're on the downtown side of a street some sane cabby would take back toward the center of town, and then walk toward the center of town yourself until you hit a hotel whose doorman is energetically flagging down or calling cabs for the good hotel guests. Slip in the hotel's side door, betake yourself to the nearest rest room, and make the repairs on your bedraggled person necessary to let someone believe you've just come down from upstairs. Then ask a bellboy or the clerk on duty the name of the doorman. As you rush out to him glancing desperately at your watch, you slip him a dollar and say, "Jimmy, could you get me a cab as fast as possible? I'm really late for an important meeting." Jimmy's job is to know what to do in an emergency like this, whether it's simply opening the door of the cab that just discharged its passengers on the curb, stepping out into the street in his raincoat under his umbrella with his trusty whistle, or even picking up the phone and putting in a special call to his buddy, the Checker Cab Company dispatcher. When it comes to getting cabs on rainy days, you couldn't be in better hands than good old Jimmy's.

# Get a Room When the Hotel's Booked

Some years ago, during the convention season, a friend of mine was stranded in Chicago by the cancellation of his flight home. He telephoned several hotels, but found everything booked. Since he couldn't stay at the airport (he's a light sleeper), he took a cab into the Loop and inquired at the Palmer House, where he had stayed often, whether any of their reservations had cancelled. The desk clerk was sympathetic but firm. "There are no rooms," he said.

"Well," said my friend, "how about some pull-out in a conference room or a closed-off portion of a connecting suite?" The clerk shook his head. My friend then asked to see the manager, who appeared and gave the same negative reply: no rooms. "I know it's practice," my friend confided to the manager, "to keep a few rooms back. Let me take one. I'll pay the price of a suite."

"I'm sorry, sir," the manager replied. "We have no such rooms."

They always have such rooms, and my friend knew it. "You mean to say," he smiled, "that if the President of the United States came in now and asked for a room, you would refuse him?"

The manager, restraining a chuckle, admitted, "I suppose we would have to come up with a room for the President."

"Well," my friend brightened, "Lyndon Johnson happens to be in Texas tonight. Would you give me *his* room?"

My friend got his room, finally, at 3:00 A.M., when a vacancy occurred. What wit had not been able to secure, patience had, for he had got the room eventually, just by waiting around.

And that is the principal secret of getting a room at a "booked" hotel: wait until the situation changes. At midnight the manager may be quite reluctant to cancel a late arrival's reservation to accommodate you. But an hour or two later, he will begin to consider more seriously the possibility that the Kuwaiti playboy who has reserved Suite 69 will turn out to be a no-show. At this point he will look up to see you still dozing in the lobby, and you will begin to look very good to him. At 3 o'clock in the morning, from his perspective, a bird in the hotel is worth any number in the logbook.

If you have gone out of your way to make the clerk remember you, of course, it will be an added advantage. One strategy always works for me. When the desk clerk tells me there are no rooms, I engage him in light conversation for a few moments, making sure to get his name. Then I excuse myself and, after a few more minutes, return with an envelope I have addressed to him. In it I leave a note. "I am eating in the hotel restaurant and would appreciate being told if any vacancies occur." I also enclose a five- or ten-dollar bill.

As I hand him the note, I say, "Mr. Hodges, I will be eating in the Empire Room for the next couple of hours. Would you please inform the switchboard, since I may be getting a few calls from Washington. And please notify me if there is a sudden cancellation."

Since no hotel is full of prepaid reservations, and there are always cancellations, hotels as a rule open up reserved rooms when the guests are more than a couple of hours late. This is particularly so after 8:00 P.M. At that time, a clerk who has received a small gratuity is already inclined in your favor; if a room does become available, you will get the first nod. And the clerk, incidentally, feels no chicanery here. You haven't bribed him, you have only tipped him for helping direct that call to you in the dining room. After all, it may be from the White House.

# Get Your Hotel Room Changed

One extremely finicky socialite I know once ended up in a posh resort with a hotel room whose toilet did not flush quite properly. After three fruitless calls to the desk requesting that a bellboy be sent up immediately to remove her and her belongings to some decently civilized premises, she decided there was only one way to get action. So she went downstairs, staggered up to the desk, and loudly told the manager—and a half a dozen people who were just checking in—"If I can't get my room changed immediately, I'm checking out of this hotel!"

"But madame!" The manager rushed around the desk to hush her up, seeing that if she created a nuisance he would have half a dozen more empty rooms than he'd planned on that night. "What do you claim is wrong with your room?"

"Well, for one thing," she proclaimed, "the toilet doesn't flush quite properly. And for another thing, it's on fire."

# Get Tickets to "Sold Out" Broadway Shows

What do you do when the Broadway show everyone is talking about is booked for the next four months?

First, consider that banks, advertising agencies, and the media all reserve first-run tickets. If you've paid back your auto loan on time, or know somebody who knows somebody who works for Ogilvy and Mather or CBS, check out those angles: maybe your friend of a friend really can get you into front row center the night after tomorrow. If you're in Little Rock and want tickets to some sold-out sensation for your trip to the Big Apple in two weeks, your best bet is to ask your banker whether he has a corresponding New York bank that can handle it for you.

If not, you do have other options, if you're in The City. One is to deal with the scalpers. Most of these—certainly the visible ones—are on the street, hanging around in front of all major theatres like the Lyceum or the Eugene O'Neill, an hour before curtain time. Others have plush offices and supply the big New York companies with instant box seats for out of town clients. Both these sources have a common drawback, and that is that they will end up charging you forty dollars for a ten-dollar ticket.

Gamblers might like to hoof it to the Times Square Center on Forty-second Street a few hours before curtain time and check the last-minute situation; not only are tickets often available, they are often half-price. Or you can wait around the box office for last-minute no-shows, which quite often works.

Finally, you can call Joseph Papp, director of the American Shakespeare Festival and entrepreneur for some of New York's best-known productions, and say you are anxious to become a patron of the festival.

A fifty-dollar supporter's fee buys not only the gratification of having helped out one of the nation's finest struggling theater companies, but the opportunity to purchase tickets to any of Mr. Papp's many Broadway and off-Broadway productions. Including one you may have heard of: *A Chorus Line*.

# Get Cheap or Free Hotel Rooms for Lunchtime Trysts

A few years ago, I had to borrow the office of a friend while mine was being painted. Rummaging in his drawers for paper clips, I came upon a large pile of local hotel keys. "Why?" I asked when he stopped by. "Do you collect room keys?"

"Oh," he answered casually, "I hate to pay the rate for a room when I'm only going to use it for an hour or so. If I have a lunch date, sometimes I'll go to one of the hotels with sandwiches and wine. One of the keys is certain to be to an unoccupied room. No problems with maids—I'm always out by the check-out time."

I admired his ingenuity, but for those of us who are wary of risking detection as suspected hotel thieves or vagrants, there is a more conventional, though obviously not as cheap, way to get a room for those special few hours. Most hotels have day rates which are seldom much more than half the regular price of the room. I have used them often to freshen up in the interval between a plane landing and an evening speaking engagement. A simple inquiry about day rates may lead to the pleasant surprise that you don't in fact have to sell the limo in order to afford lunches in Plaza suites.

# Crash an Exclusive Reception

You read about it in the social pages. A dinner reception at The Club Room in honor of the First Baronet of Malmsey, in town to finalize plans for his endowment of the Anglo-American Saltwater Skydiving Fund. The guest list, three hundred strong, includes the cream of the international sherry set—everybody who has ever shaken a lorgnette at a waiter. You decide you must be there. But how?

The answer is simple. Nerve.

In a reception this size, there are bound to be a few empty seats. Assuming the identity of a missing guest for the evening will get you not only a free dinner, but the chance to rub shoulders with luminaries of true rank and privilege. All you have to do is get inside. Once you are seated and chatting, the combination of sherry and the speakers' fustian will ensure that not even the missing person's brother will realize you are not him.

But how do you get in? Well, being nervy enough to crash a fancy affair does involve more than simple arrogance. Bluster and push will only get you thrown out. It's a blend of previous planning and a certain steely aplomb that will get you in.

So: prepare. Put on a tuxedo, since a black tie will convince the door guards you are either at the head table or a waiter. Wear a button that says "Host" or "Finance Committee." Carry a notebook. Sling a tape recorder or camera around your neck. Above all, look as if you know what you're doing. More potential crashers have been stopped by a shifty eye than all other giveaways combined. Become convinced that you belong. Remember that you outrank the guards, and unless you give them an excuse to question your presence—such as ogling dignitaries with a stunned expression on your face—it will never occur to them to do so.

Most important of all, Don't Stop. Look straight·ahead, and walk with determination—don't run. If there's a check-in table, ignore it. You are in a hurry to introduce the Baronet, and you have no time for such foolishness.

Should you be stopped, look irritated, as if the functionary interrupting your progress has just aborted the Message to Garcia. Announce that you've been paged and are expected at the podium. (Someone has always just been paged, and chances are only the pagee has heard the name.) Stand on your dignity. Refuse to be intimidated by underlings. Many a crasher, confusing apprehension with having been found out, displays embarrassment at this point and goes out looking sheepish.

This is all wrong, the result of poor preparation. If you have truly convinced yourself that you belong inside, the marshals will pick up on your confidence, assume that any mistake being made is their own, and beg you to remain.

As a last resort, pull rank. Finger your black tie, allow an air of aristocratic ennui to descend, and hint that, if this travesty continues, you will withdraw the Baronet's endowment.

# Get Drinks on the House

Years ago there was a journeyman pitcher in the major leagues nicknamed Eagle Eye. His teammates called him that not for his mound delivery, but for his extraordinary ability to find stones, shells, bones, and other foreign matter in his food whenever he ate at a restaurant. Upon spotting some of this apparently ubiquitous debris in the last few bites of his broccoli, *boeuf bourguignon,* or whatever, he would call first the waiter and then the maître d' to the table, and expostulate loudly about the sorry state of the kitchen. The maître d' would offer to give him another entree, but Eagle Eye would shake his head and say, "I've lost my appetite now. Just give me a drink." Occasionally, toying with

141

extortion, he would claim that in discovering the nugget he had cracked his bridgework or nearly gagged to death. Many a maître d' anxious to avoid further publicity allowed the pitcher to get drunk on the house.

Personally, I prefer the carrot approach to the stick approach. In a good restaurant, you can ask the waiter if the chef would mind autographing the menu so you can keep it as a souvenir of an overwhelming culinary experience. Such flattery nearly always wins a drink on the house.

In all pubs in the British Isles and Ireland—and in those American bars where the traditions of the Auld Sod are maintained—it is the custom for the bartender to buy a regular drinker one complimentary round for each three or four he has purchased, even if he's not a regular customer, or has never been there before. To find a bar with this delightful practice—the free drinks are called "buy-backs," which is nice because it suggests you've earned them—look for shamrocks, especially in working-class Irish neighborhoods. After you've quaffed a few, the free drink will be placed before you with a soft-spoken, "Good luck." (If, after half a dozen drinks, you are beginning to squint mournfully at the bartender and he shows no signs of coming across, forget it and try another bar.)

Finally, there are numerous establishments that advertise, as a way of drumming up business, one or two free drinks with a meal. These offers are generally good value, if you don't mind eating with your booze. Almost as good are the Happy Hours during which all drinks are reduced, and the All You Can Drink come-ons, where for, say, five dollars, you can sit at the bar from nine to midnight and imbibe to your heart's content. The theory is that few drinkers will drink more than the cover, but it is not really very hard to become one of that few. Do not, however, expect to be served Chivas Regal. Invariably such deals exclude the more expensive and imported brands.

# Reach Friends with Unlisted Phone Numbers

Suppose you want to reach a friend or acquaintance about something you are sure she would want to hear about, but you call information and to your frustration—"unlisted."

There is no way on earth you are going to get that number out of the phone company, but if you are determined enough, you can probably get your friend on the phone.

First, don't overlook the obvious possibility that your friend may have given her number to other friends. Call mutual acquaintances, your friend's employer, parents, siblings. If none of them knows the number, perhaps one of them would suggest someone else to call. If one of them knows the number but will not give it to you, ask if he will call your friend and have her call you if she wants. I once called seven parties until contacting an inaccessible friend's ex-wife, who, it turned out, knew where he could be reached.

In emergencies it is possible to reach an unlisted party through the operator. If you convince the operator that your case, even if not a matter of life or death, is at least desperate enough to merit serious attention, an operator (usually a special one you are transferred to) may call your party directly, relay your message, and have her call you back.

But if the nature of your message would show the operator that this isn't a "real" emergency, of course you can't mention it—so you try telling the operator it is highly confidential, or too personal, or whatever else works.

More elaborate ploys have been known to bypass even the most hardbitten of operators. You might, for example, go to a jail or hospital and from its pay phone ask the operator to get you the Attendant Supervisor. Tell her, "I am James Humes, Deputy Assistant Commissioner,

143

and I must reach Mrs. Elizabeth Cavanaugh of 87 Park Lane. Will you have her call me as soon as possible? I am at St. Theresa's Hospital." And give the hospital number. Be brief and don't answer any questions.

When Mrs. C. calls back, *remember that the telephone company operator may be monitoring.* Tell her you cannot talk right now, ask for her number, and say you will call *her* back in a few minutes. This will prevent the company from discovering the nature of your "emergency."

# Lend Books and Get Them Back

One of the late editors of the *Saturday Evening Post* had the only foolproof system for lending books. To maintain his extensive library, he had to find a polite way to impress on borrowers their obligation to return books. When a friend asked to take home a book, he would bring down from his shelf a black notebook. The borrower would then have to write in the space provided the book title, along with her name, address, phone number, and the date of lending. When a book was kept out too long a time, he would call the person and say, "I'm sorry to ask this, but I'm working on an article and need that book you have."

# Get a Table Down Front

We were tired and hungry. The committee meeting had got out at half past nine, and it was half past ten before we made it to the restaurant. We had no desire to spend the next thirty minutes in the fresh air, but we saw no way of breaking through the four hundred people ahead of us short of outright bribery.

So we used bribery.

One member of our group, a Southern boy dressed conservatively in a tweed three-piece suit with white handkerchief and tie, happened to be perfectly equipped to approach the maître d'. He went up to this already much-harassed worthy and flashed a small black leather case, embossed in gold with a U.S. Treasury seal. "Pierre," he said with as much nonchalance as he could muster, "we really are in a fix for a table." Then he opened the case and slowly detached a pair of five-dollar bills from a whole pad of them, which were bound together like so many single five-dollar postage stamps.

Pierre's eyes bulged at the exquisitely tantalizing "rrrrrikk" that detached one five-dollar bill from our friend's personal pack of perforated greenbacks.

Actually, it's not at all difficult to purchase one of these maître d' stoppers. They are available—fresh from the engraver and already attached to their folder—from many of our major banks. Ask around your town. Do not settle for imitations. In a pinch, have your bank write to the Bank of Nevada.

But if you don't want to invest in such an expensive come-on, you might employ more traditional gambits, such as the envelope slipped discreetly to the maître d' when others in line are not looking. Be sure to enclose at least a ten. Then wait, as if you are slumming royally on the sidelines, until Pierre comes up to nod you to the front. In big nightspots the unrecorded tip is bread and butter both for the maître d' and for the various minions under his jurisdiction, so don't underestimate the power of such a bribe.

If you don't like to tip, you can always try titles. "The Judge's hearing's not too good," you might say. "We need a table closer to the front." Or try, "The Ambassador's eyes are failing. Could we please have a front table?"

Whatever you do, watch out when you use the term Governor. Once at a dinner club in Atlantic City I announced myself as "Governor Humes" and the maître d' insisted on having the band play our state song. "What state, Governor?" he asked. Flustered, I came out with "the Virgin Islands," and for the next twenty minutes I was regaled with the dulcet tones of steel drums and the lilting incomprehensibility of Island patois.

# Deal with the Wine Steward

The protocol of serving wine, long shrouded in misty tradition, has been known to intimidate more than one fledgling guest of Delmonico's or the Tour d'Argent. As if the arcana of merely selecting the wine were not hurdle enough, the novice must, in these bastions of the raised eyebrow, contend as well with a whole etiquette covering what happens between the removal of the bottle from the cellar to the actual drinking. The focus of this etiquette is the sommelier, or wine steward, who in the best of places still wears the leather jerkin and the small silver *taste vin* (literally "wine taster") signifying his profession.

Traditionally the steward himself tasted the chosen bottle before offering it to the host. Nowadays diners are seldom nervous about an enemy in the kitchen, perhaps because public poisoning has declined in popularity, so this formality is dispensed with and the host takes the trial sip himself. This central moment of the ritual is often seen by the uninitiated host as an opportunity for him to accept or reject the wine on the basis of whether or not he likes it. This is not the purpose of the exercise. You have chosen the wine after all, and the steward has gone to the trouble of uncorking the bottle, so for all practical purposes you are stuck with your choice.

What you are being asked to judge is merely whether or not the particular bottle selected is still sound, or has gone "off." Unless the liquid turns your nose into a corkscrew, you should simply nod to the steward, who will then fill your and the other diners' glasses. If you believe the wine is sour, the steward will then taste it himself, and either confirm or question your judgment. Do not be shy about speaking up. While restaurants are understandably reluctant to change wines with their customers' whims, there is no point to being intimidated into drinking vinegar.

Aside from the actual tasting, there are a few smaller mysteries con-

146

fronting the novice. Often, before pouring the wine, the sommelier will offer the extracted cork to the host. This is not a souvenir. He is expecting you to examine it to assure yourself it is still in one piece, and that it smells, again, of wine and not vinegar. Or, the steward might decant an old bottle of wine into a carafe, holding it in front of a candle flame so it may be seen better. He is inviting you to make sure, with him, that no sediment is allowed to enter the carafe. In the case of white wines, the steward—in those rare places where prechilling has not already become the norm—will immerse the bottle in crushed ice at your table and expect you to tell him, after feeling the neck, when it is cold enough to pour.

Occasionally an unscrupulous establishment passes off cheap wine, in a carafe or a mislabelled bottle, as the real stuff. If you know enough about wine to be able to say *with certainty* that the wine you are being asked to taste is not the wine you ordered, say so. Although I am not an authority on wines, I do know Beaujolais from rosé, and in London a few years back I had the distinct pleasure of sending a huffy waiter back to the kitchen with a carafe of mock Beaujolais; if you know you are correct, no reputable restaurant will disagree. If, however, you are uncertain, it is better to hold your peace and drink the dregs.

# Start Your Own Wine Cellar

Nothing has quite the old-world ring of the phrase, "my wine cellar." Somehow it's a comforting thought: all those bottles lying down there on their sides, their contents aging and improving away steadily on their own while you are painting your yacht or washing the dishes. The snob appeal is not to be denied either.

Now, starting a wine cellar is not exactly the cheapest thing in the world to do if you really want to get into it right; whereas if you merely want to talk about your wine cellar (to people who'll never ask to see it), you can do that for the price of throwing an old bottle of sherry you never drink down the cellar steps.

But let's assume for the fun of it that you actually enjoy wine, realize that you can have fun collecting it (just like stamps and coins) *and* drinking it (unlike stamps and coins). Let's further suppose you have a few hundred dollars, or maybe a few thousand, to buy all at once, and at great savings, wines which you may be drinking anywhere from twenty minutes to fifty years from now. Ideally you also have a dark, cool, humid part of your cellar, where the temperature is reasonably even (the optimum is a constant 55–57 degrees). The question then becomes, What should you buy?

First of all, spend the time to hunt down a really good wine store. I don't mean necessarily one with the biggest selection in town, or one whose big draw is a locked case of outrageously overpriced Burgundies along the back wall. Try to find a place where the salespeople's knowledge of wine extends beyond knowing the difference between a Burgundy and a Bordeaux, and where they have the time and the interest to talk to you about building up your cellar. Nine out of ten wine shops in the world will be happy to take your two hundred dollars and unload on you that case of dusty-on-the-outside, musty-on-the-inside Corton that they haven't been able to move since January. What you want to find is the one place in ten that respects itself, its wine, and you more than that.

When you find a place to your liking, explain the situation to the manager. Tell him how much money you have to spend, and ask his advice in putting together a case or two cases of mixed wines. The selection, of course, must reflect your own taste, but you should try for a balance among Burgundies and Bordeaux, white and red, full-bodied and light, etc. What you should aim for is a selection with as great a regional and monetary range as possible without sacrificing quality.

Use your head. Naturally, if you have only two hundred dollars to spend, you would not be wise to invest half of that amount in a single bottle of Haut Brion '59. All that would get you is one superlative, memorable drunk. Your cellar would end up pretty empty. On the other hand, it would be no wiser to blow the bill on an even hundred bottles of Ripple, because all you'd get out of that would be three months of unmemorable drunks—and still no cellar.

Keep in mind that this initial case or two should be designed to afford you a wide variety of selection; out of this selection, you will extract those labels that especially tickle your fancy and order them, on your next visit to the wine store, in greater bulk. Suppose the "exquisitely subtle" Loire Valley bottle left you cold, but you really did a turn on that Alsatian rosé. Well, when you go back to the store, stock up on the pink and leave the subtlety to those who can appreciate it. Suppose the Segur struck you as a little unripe, and the St.-Estephe as just right. Well, get a couple of bottles of the St.-Estephe for immediate consumption, and a few of the Segur to keep for a couple of years. If you continue to follow this procedure—buy a mixed selection, do your own selection within that selection, and lay up at least a third of what you buy—you should within a couple of years have stocked a reputable cellar. I don't say it will bring tears to the eyes of every sommelier on the Lutece circuit. But it will be *your* cellar—filled with your estimates of excellence—and since you're the one who'll be drinking out of it, that's all that really matters.

Above all, fight the urge to drink everything at once. The secret of a working wine cellar is to allow at least one bottle to sit there, aging in the perfect dampness under your house, for every one you are drinking upstairs.

# Plan a Dinner at a Top French Restaurant

A restaurant . . . a restaurant . . . isn't that the kind of place where you go in, pick up the menu, see what they're offering and what you want to pay, then order, and have the food brought to you? Whoever plans a restaurant meal in advance?

Well, if you are planning to make a bangup evening of it at Lutece, for instance, which is perhaps New York City's premier French restaurant, and pay something like one hundred dollars a head for it (which I have seen accomplished on more than one occasion and with very little effort), you do not want to go blundering in with your wallet streaming twenties and fifties behind you, like a bull into the Boeuf Wellington, scrape the sauce off your turbot, and throw salt on it. No more do you want to pay twice as much for your famous name, famous vintage

Bordeaux as you would for a slightly less famous wine every bit as good, which probably would go better with your food.

So before you walk into Lutece or any other first-rate French restaurant with five hundred dollars in your wallet and say, ''Give everybody two of the three most expensive things on the wine list and the five most expensive things on the menu . . .'' pick up your telephone. You have to make a reservation anyway, and for the top-flight French restaurant you'll have to do it some weeks in advance to assure yourself of the party you want. So at that time, mention to the person who takes the reservation that you'll be wanting to talk with the maître d' about your menu and wine selection in advance. Get the maître d's name, and find out from him how *he* thinks the dinner would best be planned.

This *he* is very important, because the maître d' of a top French restaurant is expected to be more scrupulous in matters of taste and protocol than any other type of person in the world, and if you put the ball of your dinner in his court in the proper manner, he is honor bound to treat you as royally as though you were a spy sent by his boss to find out whether he's doing his job right. So he will say something like, ''Well, if you're coming on Saturday night, sir, I suggest you call to make the final plans on Thursday afternoon. We'll know by then whether we can get good wild strawberries. . . .'' And so on.

Now if you really don't know a damned thing about planning a gourmet dinner, let alone about wine, by the time you call him back on Thursday afternoon, you're in a position to say, ''Look, Pierre, I've got to get a plane out of here in twenty minutes, so I really don't have time to do the planning I would have liked. But I know you know how to plan a dinner, or you wouldn't be where you are. So I wonder whether you'd just do me the favor of planning it for me.''

You have just asked an artist to ply his trade for you; an acrobat to show off. If you tell him how many people are coming, that you've got seventy-five dollars per person to spend, more or less (or whatever your budget is), and you'd like his suggestions for the meal and wines, he can do off the top of his head in three minutes what it would take you ten years to master. ''After all,'' you say to him as you're about to leave for the airport, ''you know the chef's specials, and you know your own wine cellar, so I'm sure at this point you can do better for my money than I can.'' You then arrange to call him back some time later and have him read his suggested menu.

When you do call him back, you will hear things like, "I thought champagne would be better than Sauterne with the wild strawberries . . . they'll be coming in tomorrow morning . . . and I strongly recommend the Château Snobappeal '59 over the Mouton '59. It's a much better value." All you do is agree with him (unless you have any real reason not to), as long as he's got the kind of dinner you envisioned within the budget you gave him.

But do watch out. If he says, "Well, sir, I believe the ideal menu for your party would be one Nedick's hot dog charred to a cinder by our chef and a warm, yellow drink produced by our busboy during one of his forty-second breaks"—you'll know your budget wasn't high enough.

Of course if you know enough about fine food and/or wine to discuss with Pierre whether the paté or the steamed mussels would go equally well with the particular chablis he suggests (or even to say you'd rather not have chablis with paté), or whether the Lafite '45 should be opened at two or three in the afternoon, in view of the fact that one of your guests might be late, then go to it. As long as you know what you're talking about, Pierre will be glad to talk to you. But if you don't, as long as you compliment and tip Pierre generously for his truly extraordinary services, you will be welcomed back for as many lessons in how to plan a dinner at a top French restaurant as you can afford.

# Mix the Perfect Martini

The actor John Barrymore was a great connoisseur of the martini. Once, in the Players' Club in New York, he asked for his usual 10-to-1 martini and was shocked when the new bartender asked, "Shall I twist a bit of lemon over it, sir?"

"My good fellow," said Barrymore, "when I want lemonade, I'll ask for it."

The story illustrates the remarkable finickiness of most martini drinkers. I have known people who would drink no martini drier than a solid 8-to-1, and I have known others who feel that the proper recipe for the perfect drink is two ounces of gin and a bartender with a soft voice who whispers "vermouth" over the glass. So the mystique of the martini continues, complicated by gin-producers urging ever drier concoctions and rival businessmen suggesting such abominations as gin and bitters or white rum and vermouth.

Actually, there are only four things to remember when you set about to mix the perfect martini. One: get good gin. Two: get good vermouth. Three: mix in the proper proportions. And four: keep it cold.

Among gins I rate Boodles first, followed closely by Bombay and Tanqueray. A distant but respectable fourth is Gordon's, the most popular gin in America. All others you can forget about. As for vermouth, stick with Boissiere and you can't go wrong. Noilly Prat will do in a pinch, but for reverse snobbism choose Stock, a less expensive but flawless vermouth. For a different kind of martini experience, try some Russian vodka topped with Blonde Lillet.

As for proportion: the purists insist that nothing sweeter than 10-to-1 should be allowed to advertise itself as a martini. Others, however, demand more than this trace additive of fragrance in their gin, and have been known to sing the praises of concoctions as sweet as 8- or even 6-to-1. What's sauce for the goose is not necessarily sauce for the gander.

Finally, how do you keep it cold? One way is to keep the glasses in the refrigerator in the freezer until the last second. Another is to add ice, although you must be sure to allow for dilution by making the original mixture closer to 12-to-1 than the classic 10. The Dutch drink their gin as the Russians drink their vodka—icy cold and neat. So cold, in fact, that the liquid has begun to thicken, so that it runs down your throat like some exotic motor oil—gelid, scintillating, and refined. This kind of gin, to be sure, makes a lousy martini, but a hell of a good shot in the dark.

# Put Down Scotch Whisky Snobs

When I was a schoolboy in England, I once attended a luncheon given by Prince Philip, the Duke of Edinburgh. I wore a gray flannel suit, a white shirt, and—in recognition of my Scottish ancestry—a Royal Stuart plaid tie. During the reception, Philip cocked an eye at the tartan and said to me, "I'm glad to see an American who is proud of his Scotch background."

Now, my schoolteacher mother had taught me early on the difference between "Scotch" and "Scottish," so I hastened to set my host straight.

"Sir," I said, "as you well know, Scotch is a liquid. My heritage is Scottish."

"Young man," replied the Duke, "I rather think you're right. But I venture to say that more Scotch flows in American veins than Scottish."

Well, the Duke was right. A lot of Scotch does flow in American veins. But it's seldom the same kind of Scotch that flows in veins across the Atlantic, and to keep up with Scotch snobs, Scottish or not, you should know about a major distinction. The British and Scottish are fond of the heavier brands—Teacher's, Dewar's, Haig, Ballantine—while the Americans prefer light mixtures. Cutty Sark and J&B, the most popular American brands, are seldom drunk in the British Isles. American cocktail parties are full of boors insisting that Chivas Regal (or Johnny Walker Black) is "the finest Scotch in the world." If you are ever confronted with one of these creatures, you might simply pull out your stiffest brogue and point out that it hardly seems worthwhile to pay exorbitant rates for a blend that—whatever its virtues over the pedestrian J&B—is still "absolutely anemic compared with a malt."

Perhaps the snob will know about malts, but if he's an American it's unlikely. So enlighten him. Tell him that the essence of any good Scotch is pure malt whisky. This whisky is blended with neutral grain spirits in varying ratios to produce a range of different "blended Scotches." A high proportion of spirits yields the strongly alcoholic but relatively tasteless blends favored by Americans. A high proportion of the malt yields the less potent but infinitely more robust drinks popular across the ocean. "If all you want to do is get drunk," you might snicker, "I suppose Chivas Regal is fine."

When he demands to know which brand *you* drink, suck at your Teacher's and say that you cannot, alas, afford to indulge in the whisky you would really like to be drinking. But if you had the money, you would drink nothing but straight, *unblended* single malts. If he keeps pressing for a name, look puzzled and reply, "Oh, Glenlivet, Glenfiddich, Glendronach Laphroaig—surely you are familiar with the great malts?"

Whatever your snob claims, he should be made to see that, across the Atlantic where Scotch distilling began, his tastes would seem hopelessly provincial. Real Scotch lovers (which is to say, Scottish Scotch lovers) will settle for nothing but the pure, unblended malt. I have known aficionados to sip it neat, like cognac, after dinner. The single malt *is* Scotch. Anything else, say the purists, is only alcohol.

And remember, incidentally—never, never write "whisky" with an *e*. The Scotch—whoops, Scottish—say that it stands for "English."

# Put Down Bourbon Snobs

At least in my experience, bourbon snobs are even more unbearable than Scotch snobs. Perhaps it only looks that way to me because while I'm relatively untutored on sourmash, I do know my single malts. In any event, bourbon drinkers seem to me as a class outrageous in their claims to have gotten the latest inside track on the "bourbon of the century." You know the characters I mean. At parties they're always slumped in a corner somewhere crying out for branch water and nasalizing the end of "bourbon" so it comes out sounding like "boor-bone." It does not seem to matter whether they are Yankee or Rebel, rich or poor. Park Avenue executives will announce with utter conviction that Wild Turkey is the quintessence of the bourbon experience, while an Alabama sharecropper will insist with no less conviction that the only decent bourbon in the nation is made by his cousin Huck in the next county.

I suppose that no matter what I say here, the debate over Wild Turkey versus Jack Daniels versus Dickel will go on. So I only want to throw out a little basic information about the drink, and to relate an anecdote that will show you how, the next time a snobbish guest suggests that your bourbon stock is second-rate, you can show him up for the dummy he doubtless is.

Bourbon is distilled from a combination of cornmash, malt, and rye and aged in oak barrels until it is ripe. "Ripeness" is of course a matter of personal taste, but most bourbon fanciers seem to agree that eight to ten years is the minimum time the potion should stay in the cask before being drawn out and bottled. Bourbon that has aged in the barrel for twelve to fifteen years is therefore highly prized (and highly priced). Generally speaking, it is difficult to find a bourbon with over fifteen years of aging on the commercial market: any brew with that distinction has long ago become some connoisseur planter's private stock. If you do turn up such a gem in a speciality liquor store, it is likely to run you twenty bucks a bottle.

Remember that bourbon, unlike wine, does not improve in the bottle. So if somebody uncaps a bottle of twelve-year-old Dickel, drink it *now*. Conversely, if Cousin Clem from Pemmican Junction sent you a fruit jar full of sourmash last Christmas, and your first taste suggested a cross between molten lead and motor oil, don't keep it on the shelf in the hopes it will be better next Christmas. Use it on the charcoal fire now. (Straight "sourmash" or "corn likker" is distilled much the same way as bourbon, but without the leavening agents malt and rye. Since the time allowed for this potent brew to mellow in the cask is far, far short of eight years, it is not surprising that its most common alias is "White Lightning.")

If you're confronted by a bourbon snob, then, keep in mind the process that goes into making a fine bourbon and get one up on him. This is what a friend of mine did at a recent party. A midwestern

155

Congressman, condescending to drink my friend's Jack Daniels, had suggested that, fine as it was, it "just wasn't Dickel." My friend drew him aside.

"Listen," my friend said. "I didn't realize you were such a bourbon connoisseur. Why don't you come down to the cellar with me for a minute? I've got a little something I think you might be interested in sampling."

On the way down the steps he explained that a couple of months ago he had cleaned up at a poker game, relieving a Cotton-Belt Congressman of not only a sizable billfold but also a case of his private stock bourbon. It had been "bottled in bond" for the unlucky gentleman, and was reputed to have been aged for seventeen years, six months, and a day. The guest's eyebrows went up.

"I see no reason to waste this elixir on people who wouldn't appreciate it," he explained. "You of course are an exception."

And there my friend had him. He guzzled down his "private stock" as if it were ambrosia itself, and allowed as how it was, indeed, the finest bourbon he'd ever encountered. My friend didn't tip the phony off, and as far as I know to this day he is still unaware that the drink he preferred to his Dickel was bottled originally in a fruit jar in Pemmican Junction.

# Savor a Cigar like a Churchillian Connoisseur

Since the time of Rudyard Kipling, one of whose characters preferred East-Indies stogies to the charms of a wife, the cigar has been considered almost a weapon of male chauvinism. It has driven ladies from libraries and billiard rooms. It's strong after-reek has been the cover-up for perfume inherited from a night out on the town. Thus, many women manifest strong objections when a cigar is unsheathed from a man's pocket.

My friend Bob Smith, former Chief Counsel of the Senate Government Operations Committee, has a pat comment when he begins to precisely clip his evening cigar. "You know," he pontificates, "you can always tell a girl's breeding from the way she reacts to a cigar." "If, when she grew up, her father was always chewing on a cheroot while watching the ball game in his undershirt with a can of beer, she detests them. However, if she has memories of her father lounging in the library in his smoking jacket, slowly puffing on his cigar while he sipped his cognac, she tends to like, even love the smell of cigars."

At this point, the girl usually coughingly protests that she doesn't mind cigars or at least good ones. Actually, a cheap cigar is an abomination, hardly above the status of snuff or chewing tobacco. On the other hand, a good cigar is an exquisite delight like aged French cheese or old port.

Sir Winston Churchill once said, "A good cigar is like an exciting mistress—it needs constant attention or else the flame will die out." True, it should be lit carefully with a wooden match—letting the match burn a bit, before gently caressing the edges with the flame. Once lit, you should take pains to keep it lit; a rekindled cigar, like rekindled love, has lost some of its passion.

Like vintage wine, good cigars have their equivalent of bouquet, body, and flavor. The *bouquet* is its wrapper (the best ones are Cameroon leaves from Africa); the *body* is how it is made (does its filler allow it to burn evenly or does it tend to unravel?) Finally, the *flavor*—it is here that the Havanas are without equal. Actually the post-Castro Havanas in the nationalized factories are an uneven lot—most do not measure up to the old Havanas in terms of the hand-packing and rolling of the wrapper, filler, and tobacco.

The best cigars on the American market are made by the old cigar families who have taken their Cuban seed to more hospitable islands. The Jamaicans are often the best made but the mildest in flavor. The strongest are from Honduras. In between are the ones from the Spanish Canary Islands, which many Americans think are better than Havanas. Most cigar connoisseurs who want richness like the Honduras product. For a wrapper they prefer the ripe "maduro" (dark) or "Natural" in contrast to the "greenish" or "Claro" which is the color of many American machine-made cigars.

Whatever your taste, never buy a prepierced cigar. (Don't even mention a plastic-tip holder!) Don't inhale and don't chain smoke even if you are a millionaire. Cigars are a once-an-evening affair after dinner—preferably with brandy, port, or straight whisky. For your hostess's sake, don't leave your cigar in the ash tray—take it with you. Put it in the garbage or flush it down the toilet.

Since I assume you readers are good patriotic Americans, I strongly suggest you do what my cousin John Humes did when, as Ambassador, he received a case of Havanas. This was a sensitive problem since the United States had no diplomatic relations with Castro's Cuba. Accordingly, he gave these orders to his staff, "Burn them—slowly—one by one."

# Have the Ideal "European Experience"

Anybody can make the Grand Tour. It takes no imagination to call up a travel agent, reserve a berth on the Q.E. II (cosmopolites never say Queen Elizabeth) and suites in seven Grand Hotels, and hop into a limousine bound for the piers. But suppose you want to do something a little different this year?

Now, we Americans are a travelling people—we seem almost born to ramble. Yet we often forget that we are not alone in this: that, while we are taking our vacation in Paris, the Parisians have gone to Brittany for the summer. Why not capitalize on this little-recognized fact and arrange to house-sit or apartment-sit for an absent European? It would be a lot cheaper than a hotel, and you would get the opportunity to actually live like a European, if only for a month or two weeks.

The reference desk of any competent library should be able to give you the names of the major local newspapers in the area you want to stay. Write a brief advertisement offering your services as house-sitter, making sure to make yourself and your family sound like paragons of respectability, and send it to at least a dozen papers. If you can get the copy translated into the relevant language, so much the better, but if not, don't worry: most of the major European newspapers occasionally publish classifieds in tongues other than their own *lingua franca.*

Wherever you are hoping to stay, do not forget to place an ad in the *International Herald Tribune,* which is distributed in all the major European cities, read by both Europeans and visiting Americans, and might just land on the breakfast table of a Roman fashion designer who has been sitting up nights wondering what to do with her villa this summer.

My advice would be to focus your advertisements on the big cities and on college towns, since they are the most likely places to be the winter residences of itinerant businessmen and professors. Send the ads in early enough to allow two or three months for negotiations, and then sit back and wait for offers. With any luck, you'll end up paying a ridiculously low sublet rate and find yourself changing your official address, if only temporarily, to something with the romantic ring of "Wilhelmstrasse," "Rue du Four," or "Piazza Navona."

Which is a hell of a lot more chic than "Suite 123, Grand Hotel."

# Have an Out-Of-This-World Vacation Experience

When I first went abroad to England, an aunt took me aside and said, "Jamie, when you return, people are going to come up to you and say, 'Did you see the Crown Jewels?' and you'll say yes. Then they'll ask, 'Did you go to Stratford on Avon?' and you'll nod. Then they'll inquire, 'Did you see Stonehenge?' you'll say 'no' and they will shake their heads sympathetically and say, 'Really, that's too bad—that is the most interesting thing I saw in my whole trip.'"

"That's why," my aunt advised, "you want to choose an out-of-the-way place like Clovelly [a quaint postcard town built on a seaside cliff in Devon] and be able to come up with 'Oh, you didn't see Clovelly? That was the highlight of my whole trip.' "

Twenty-five years later, the test of a real traveler can no longer be just Britain or even Europe. Even journeys to the Middle East or Japan are common. You must pick an "out-of-this-world" spot for the vacation experience if you want to be armed with good cocktail party conversation the rest of your life.

One such place is Machu Picchu, "the Lost City of the Incas." This Peruvian mecca for jaded travelers lies 11,000 feet above sea level. No one lives there, no one works there. It is a celestial city surrounded by steaming jungle and snow-capped mountains.

In these Temples of the Andes time has stood still for centuries. To get there take a charter (O.T.C.) flight to Lima and another flight from there to Cuzco. At Cuzco let yourself adjust to the altitude by staying there for a day before taking the train ride to Machu Picchu. Although you can go up and look for a day, you can stay overnight at the Hotel Turista, a creaky hotel armed with candles and with no communication with the outside world except for a staticky short-wave radio. That gives you more time to explore the fascinations of the world's most hauntingly beautiful city.

For a more relaxing vacation, you might want to try the original Shangri-la, high in the Himalayas. Hire a house boat on Dal Lake in the exotic Vale of Kashmir. These three-bedroom boats, walled in teak and floored with Orientals, float in a crystal-clear stillness that carries gardens on its surface and reflects images of the snow-capped mountains. The mists in the early morning give such shimmering beauty and at sunset the colors are so vibrant that it's a horizon that can never be lost by your mind. To get to this cool oasis of the mountains, take the two-hour flight to Srinagar from New Delhi. Before taking a taxi to the lake, be sure to visit the Mogul garden of Shalimar, the royal abode of love.

For another top-of-the-world trek, take a trip to the land of the Midnight Sun, a journey that is less expensive but equally satisfying. There is an almost deafening silence in gliding past the stark cliffs in nightless beauty.

The nineteenth-century American violinist Ole Bull was once asked if the inspiration for his music came from his memories of seeing this end-of-the-earth cape of his native Norway. Ole replied, "No, it wasn't my eyes looking, it was my soul listening." The secret in planning this

160

North Cape cruise is not to book passage in one of the Scandinavian ocean-crossing vessels but instead go to Norway and buy a ticket on one of the smaller vessels that can explore deep the craggy nooks and crannies of the fjords. The best way is the cheapest—Royal Mail Steamer. On this smaller boat, which stops at each Norwegian fishing village, you can one-up the luxury liners, who never probe the mysteries of this Arctic top of the world.

# Hitch-Hike Across America

Twenty-five years ago, when I had just finished my freshman year at Williams, I decided to take the ultimate All-American vacation and hitch-hike across the country.

To earn money along the way I first got myself set up as a salesman for a nylon-stocking company, and I carried a sample and order forms with me to the more affluent suburban districts along the way. (Most house peddlers stay away from areas where servants are likely to answer the door.) Acting just like everyone else's young son in college, I managed to earn my expenses. Actually, I made most of my money selling to domestic help.

In the fifties my thumbing uniform was a jacket with a button-down shirt and tie. I sometimes shaved twice a day, and I carried a travel iron to make sure my clothes never looked slept-in. By today's standards such a uniform would make me look like either a "sickie" or someone who didn't really need a ride, but still, there's no doubt that the contemporary hitch-hikers with the clean jeans and the trimmer beards get the most and the best rides.

Back then we hitched only in the daytime. Nowadays you can make it at night, I hear, if you're using well-lighted roads with a lot of traffic, if you find spots where the cars are going slowly enough for the drivers to look you over, and if you make sure they've got a good, safe, legal place to pull off and pick you up.

But it is still true that if you can't bypass a city, it's damned hard to hitch-hike through it, and you're much better off spending a few cents for a bus. If you must hitch in congested areas, it's also still true that you don't stand right in front of a traffic light, but in the next block, past the intersection. You make drivers nervous by standing on top of them; but again, if they can give you a good once-over and feel you're not pushy, it's up to your appearance and your approach to make them want to stop.

When darkness fell I used to scout out the nearest truck stop, nurse coffees (with tons of sugar), and try to strike up conversations with truck drivers. It was easier to get rides with truckers then, because there weren't insurance company inspectors all over the roads in unmarked cars to enforce (among other policies) the "no riders" rule. But still, if you can get a sleepy enough trucker to trust you, he will still on occasion give you a good long ride. Your job will be to keep him awake. He figures it's better to risk running afoul of the insurance inspectors than running off the road.

If I didn't get a ride by around 11:00, I took one of two options: catch a bus for someplace where it would arrive early in the morning, or get myself a "hot pillow." This second option, especially good in small cities, involved finding a motel whose customers' cars couldn't be seen from the road—a necessary discretion for the type of night clientele that did not stay the whole night. By 2:00 or 3:00 A.M. I would invariably have spotted some couple who had signed in as Smith or Brown, paid for the room in advance, and made good their getaway. I would go in where they had gone out, and usually get an unused twin bed. In the morning I would call home person-to-person to myself, so my mother would know where I was. She could hear me (but I couldn't hear her) as I said, "Well, I'm calling from Salt Lake City, and I really would like to reach . . ." She'd always ask if the party didn't want to speak to her instead, with the charges reversed. I never did.

Another alternative I learned about was to go to the local jailhouse for lodging. I caught onto it one night in Colorado, after the state police had picked me up, thinking I was a drug user, and stripped me searching for needle marks. When they were done I asked them if I could sleep in a jail cell. They agreed. Thereafter, when I was stuck for a place to crash, I betook me to the local jailhouse, where the officials were usually quite hospitable.

Although twenty-five years have passed since then, I have learned from my nieces and other modern-day cross-country experts that most of the old rules of getting along on the road still apply. Hitch-hikers should be young, clean, and wholesome if they want to appeal to the vast majority of the traffic. A gimmick helps. Sometimes it is a guitar: if you are carrying a valuable instrument yourself, you are unlikely to rob anyone else. And you have artistic sensitivity. I have heard of people who choose guitar cases for their suitcases for this very reason. Sometimes it is a sign that does the trick. If you are going to the West Coast, "California or Bust" is an old standby. Signs that have caught my attention are, "Yale for Ford" and "We Sing for Our Supper." My best luck in hitch-hiking was a stint through Washington and Idaho in my kilt with a sign, "Too Scottish to Pay."

The one thing you have to look out for nowadays, by all reports, is getting hopelessly stuck by not using your head. If you are hitching the length of Interstate 80 through Pennsylvania and make the mistake of accepting a ride to the Woodchuck Junction Interchange, you might see one car an hour and stay there from now until eternity. You're better off staying where you are if there's decent traffic coming through and making sure your next ride takes you to someplace you can get out of.

Everyone who has ever hitch-hiked across the U.S.A. has dozens upon dozens of stories to tell about this cheapest of all possible vacations. Hitch-hiking is wonderful because you meet so many interesting people and see so much of the country. (Although the place you're most likely to remember is the place where you got stuck for six hours in the rain.)

In Illinois I was picked up by a man who had seen Lincoln. No, he hadn't been around since 1865; but in the early 1900s the grave of the martyred President was opened so the casket could be moved, and in the course of the operation the casket was also opened. My benefactor's father had been one of the workers at the graveside, and he had sent a message down to his son's grade school that he should come up on his bicycle for the momentous event. He told me Lincoln's face was the color of bronze, and his head hung back.

In Sacramento a blonde in a blue convertible picked me up, and we got along so well that she took me out to dinner at the Top of the Mark in San Francisco.

I did, however, get a real fright when a bunch of carnies picked me up in Iowa. One bottle of cheap wine and a few questions about how much money I had were enough to make me jump out as soon the car stopped for a light.

# Get "In" at New York's "21" Club

Back in the 1950s, in the heyday of the televised hearings of the Kefauver Investigations Committee on Organized Crime, a well-known Senator was questioning a certain Mafioso about his whereabouts. "At what time did you leave the '23' Club?" "Now how many of you were at the conference at the '20' Club?" "Who was it you saw at the "22" Club?" Afterward an aide caught up with him. "Senator, you were on national television, and you couldn't get the name of the '21' Club straight? We've been there together many times!" "I know," whispered the Senator, "but these days a politician can't afford to be too knowledgeable about things like that."

Well, anyone who is knowledgeable is aware that since the days of Prohibition the "21" Club has been the rendezvous of sportsmen, statesmen, actors, and authors. The club, which takes its name after its address (21 West Fifty-second Street), is not private, but it has its own way of dealing with those who are not "members" or regulars. If you are lucky enough to be given a table when you call for a reservation, you may find yourself banished to outer Siberia when you go upstairs to eat.

There are places to see and be seen at "21," and they vary according to the time of day. At lunch time, a premier people-watching position is a banquette on the second floor in the front. But if you come in with the after-theater crowd, you want to sit downstairs in the grille next to the bar.

If you are not often in New York, there is one way to become a "member"—pay fifty dollars to be on their so-called membership and mailing list. For this you receive a card with a number as well as a Christmas catalogue of some interesting gifts sold on the first floor at the Iron Gate. Such a card guarantees you a reservation and, if you go there more than once in a blue moon, recognition by its raspy-voiced owner, Peter Kriendler.

There is another, less expensive route. A girl in New Jersey persuaded several of her friends that they ought to get together and have a big bash at the "21" Club. They agreed and she kindly offered to make arrangements. She saw Kriendler personally to book the party, with the result that her name is immediately recognized when she calls.

Others who want to be "in" at the "21" Club give to Kriendler's favorite charity, the U.S. Olympic Fund. When you are downing one at the bar, ask the bartender if you can see Mr. Kriendler about the Olympic Fund, then write out a check for twenty-five dollars—it's tax deductible. But don't try to do as one person I heard about—he borrowed his cousin's Olympic jacket, which was sizes too big for him. He just got stares at the door.

# Be "In" at the Polo Bar of the Beverly Hills Hotel

Early this year a young lady called me for a special favor. She wanted me to phone her at precisely six o'clock Eastern Standard Time—three o'clock in Los Angeles, and at the Polo Bar in the Beverly Hills Hotel. Of course she had nothing to talk to me about, but once Johnnie of old Philip Morris fame, or any of the other bellboys, announces your name and brings you a portable phone, you know by the looks of the other Polo Bar Loungers that you have arrived.

The neo-Spanish luxury hotel is Hollywood at its quintessence, and the Polo Lounge is its heart. For people-watching fun, few places in America can compare with it. Watch an actor in an ascot and dark glasses slam down a phone angrily and yell, "I just won't act in such trash!" Most likely he is unemployed, and has just broken the eardrum of someone at his own answering service.

Never mind. There are real biggies to see here—the Cary Grants, John Waynes, Loretta Youngs, and so many faces vaguely familiar because of TV's rerun movies. Just sitting with a companion and guessing at who is who is worth the price of a few expensive drinks.

By the way, unless you have a super tan and a gorgeous body, don't dress Hollywood. Men shouldn't be afraid of conservative business suits or blazers and gray trousers. Women should try tailored pants suits and even dresses. To Hollywood veterans, those at the Polo Lounge are divided into three types—"we," "they," and "nobody." The "we" are film industry people. The "they" are the eastern moneymen and their TV and advertising colleagues. The "nobodies" are sightseers— not worth impressing. Since you won't be recognized as one of the movie set, at least look like a crack New York executive who might be looking for talent or meeting for a contract signing.

It is easy to create that impression if you dress the right way and befriend the bartender. Not only will he be a source of information about the comings and goings of various notables, but if you're suitably vague about your reasons for being in Los Angeles, he'll just assume you're someone important from the East. If, following an afternoon of drinking, you want to eat at Chasen's, talk to the doorman out front, and he'll get you a driver and limousine for not much more than the price of a cab. The doorman at the Beverly Hills is worth cultivating. As one of the great doormen of America, he knows more secrets than the FBI and CIA put together.

# Go to P. J. Clarke's in New York like a New Yorker

P. J. Clarke's on New York's Third Avenue is the world's most famous hamburger pub. It's more than just a great spot to eat and drink—it's a place to meet people and to be met. But you cannot simply walk in; you have to know the protocol.

Like Caesar's Gaul, P.J.'s is divided into three parts—the front (where the bar is), the middle (a dining area), and a back room. The front is for talking, the middle for watching, and the back . . . well, forget the back, because it's like Siberia—strictly for those in New York for the first time.

If you are alone, stand at the bar in the three-deep line. You are bound to meet people. Just to reach for a drink, you will have to offer at least three "excuse me's." But if you would like to see celebrities such as Jackie O., George Plimpton, or Gloria Steinem, try to sit at a table in the middle room. Whatever you do, do *not* let yourself get ushered into the back room. Instead, have a drink at the bar and eat one of the short-order hamburgers available just in back of you.

If you want to make sure that you are seated in the middle room, wear evening dress—as if you have just come from the opera or a concert. A business suit suggests that you're just a businessman from Iowa, and in P.J.'s there are really only two modes of dress: black tie or blue jeans.

# Go to Washington's Sans Souci and Not Look like a Tourist

Of all the restaurants in America, there is none harder to make a reservation for than the Sans Souci at lunch time. Even if you're a Senator calling from the Floor or a Presidential Assistant phoning from the White House there is no guarantee, unless Paul de Lisle, the maître d', personally knows you. Paul, the genial Marseilles host, has been privy to more of the powerful than Henry Kissinger. Some have even suggested him for President, but Paul demurs. "Why should I step down from the post I have?"

But for my own part I can say Paul has taken care of me since my first White House days in 1969—even though I have occasionally let him down. Once an acquaintance called me to ask if I would phone Paul and make reservations for a Saturday night. I told him that evenings weren't too difficult and inquired the name of the party. "The King and Queen of Sikkim" was the reply. "You mean you called in their behalf and you couldn't get a reservation?" "That's right," answered the caller. So I phoned the Sans Souci. "Paul," I said, "two old friends of mine are in town this weekend. I have always told them that yours is the best restaurant." "Mr. Humes, you are so kind," replied Paul. "What night is it for and what is their name?" "For Saturday, Paul," I said, "and it's the King and Queen of Sikkim." "Oh, yes," said Paul, not missing a beat. "Any friends of yours are friends of mine." But unfortunately the King and Queen pulled a "no-show" and went to another American institution—MacDonalds.

Actually it's not so difficult to make a reservation at Sans Souci if you make it at night and a couple days in advance. Various ruses have been tried at lunch time, some of them successful. A secretary named Hodges whose boss had promised to take her there if she could make the booking called for and got a reservation for Secretary Hodges. A midwestern visitor announced himself as Chairman Eaton (he was Chairman of his city's clean-up committee). The best way if you are a tourist is to ask your Congressman to make a reservation for you. Do it at least a week in advance.

Then look like you belong. It's not that difficult. Everyone else in Washington is from somewhere else too. When you people-watch (everyone does—that's why many go there), look as if you've met the people. Wave and smile, and they will nod back genially. They're pretending they know everybody too. It's quite amusing to see Nelson Rockefeller walk in and wave at some banker from Des Moines, sitting in a back corner, as though he knew him. Lobbyists who want to impress their clients do the same thing. It works every time. Just look like somebody they *should* all know.

One girl I know deliberately comes in after her date has been seated for five minutes so she can make a grand entrance. He rises to greet her and she gushes, "Darling, I'm *sorry* I'm *late*" as she pecks him on the cheek.

Another Washington couple who wanted to establish themselves as jet-setters arranged things so he was having a luncheon date with an attractive blonde while she came in escorted by a male companion. Under the eye of diners who knew them both, the husband went over to his wife's table and, after a perfunctory embrace, inquired about their dinner plans that evening. After such a civilized encounter, his reputation was made.

There are other games to watch in Sans Souci. Table-hopping is one. Try to identify those paying court to Art Buchwald or Joe Califano, the Secretary of HEW. If you are alert, you might catch the Senatorial Ploy in progress. It takes its name after a Senator who, while dining with a young nubile thing, suddenly spied constituents from his western state. After a discreet nudge by the Senator, the young lady took out her pad and jotted down some notes. When the check was presented, it was she who scanned the bill and opened her pocketbook. Naturally, the action disarmed the onlookers who assumed she must be a reporter interviewing for a story.

To hold your own with the Washington chic you can't order well-done roast beef washed down with a C.C. and ginger ale. Ask instead for a blonde Lillet with a twist of burnt orange. Then for the entree choose a poached bass with a bottle of Chablis, or if you prefer meat, pick the veal piccante along with some Claret. Whatever you eat don't do as I once did and stay until quarter of four. And be sure when you leave, to give Gilbert, the captain, a good cigar and tell him I send my best.